If Thou Endure It Well

NEAL A. MAXWELL

BOOKCRAFT
Salt Lake City, Utah

"I Am a Child of God" lyrics by Naomi Randall
© The Church of Jesus Christ of Latter-day Saints.
Used by permission.

Bookcraft is a registered trademark of Bookcraft, Inc.

Library of Congress Catalog Card Number: 96-83669

ISBN 1-57008-233-2

First Printing, 1996

Printed in the United States of America

CONTENTS

ACKNOWLEDGMENTS

Since much of the "plodding" on this manuscript was done in the summer, Colleen, once again, was patient and understanding with time that might have been hers.

I express appreciation to Cory Maxwell for his encouragement and helpful comments, and to George Bickerstaff, whose editing was most beneficial. My gratitude goes to my secretary, Susan Jackson, for the extra efforts she expended once again. Her patience with detail as well as her competency were both much appreciated.

I am grateful to my friend H. E. "Bud" Scruggs, who in the earliest stage provided helpful reactions and suggestions. Also to my only daughter-in-law, Karen Bradshaw Maxwell, who reviewed the manuscript when it was ready for submission to the publisher and made excellent suggestions.

Perry Cunningham and Kristen Goodman helped me with the statistical charts and trends I used earlier in a Church Educational System broadcast to young adults. Their charts were later incorporated into this book. For their accuracy and perceptivity, my gratitude is likewise expressed.

This is not an official Church publication. The author alone is responsible for the content and its limitations.

PREFACE

As a much younger man, I accepted the scripturally underscored importance of enduring to the end. But that stern requirement was only superficially appreciated back then. Life has since underscored, again and again, what a high test enduring well is for us mortals. Moreover, it isn't just for old people, nor is it just something one does near the very end of the pathway of discipleship. It is, instead, an ongoing thing which varies from season to season and from experience to experience.

As if all this were not enough in itself, the challenge of enduring in the last days includes so many added challenges in this difficult world. For instance, the trends cited in the forepart of the book are like pythons—capable of squeezing spirituality out unless they are deliberately offset by serious discipleship. Furthermore, some gospel principles, once very pervasive in western culture, now must compete with the "play-dough principles" of permissiveness. The situation makes for high adventure. Thus while the doctrine of enduring is like a diamond with many facets, this is an attempt to turn that diamond around, so that the light of the gospel can be played upon its different dimensions.

1

ENDURING
TO THE END

To endure is greater than to dare (William Makepeace Thackeray).[1]

When the Latter-day Saints make up their minds to endure, for the kingdom of God's sake, whatsoever shall come, whether poverty or riches, whether sickness or to be driven by mobs, they will say it is all right, and will honor the hand of the Lord in it, and in all things, and serve Him to the end of their lives, according to the best of their ability, God being their helper. If you have not made up your minds for this, the quicker you do so the better. (Brigham Young.)[2]

The divine direction given to a suffering Prophet Joseph Smith to *"endure* it well" should likewise entice serious disciples and cause them to examine those three precious and instructive words.

To *endure* means not only to last but also to bear up under stress, to "hold fast," even "valiantly," while maintaining the correct course set by God (see D&C 121:8, 29).

The word *it* refers to the configuration of Joseph Smith's special adversities and afflictions, which of course were added to the general challenges of mortality itself. Each of us has his own customized *it* with an ample supply of individualized tutoring and stretching challenges that are to be confronted.

The word *well* in this instance means performing with "grace under pressure" while being of good cheer, including coping with

1

indignities and afflictions, as did Job, without "[charging] God foolishly" (see Job 1:22).

The combined words *endure it well* thus connote unwearying persistence in discipleship, in fact, a "pressing forward" with "a perfect brightness of hope" (see 2 Nephi 31:20).

Following this relevant divine adjuration, "endure it well," the Prophet Joseph was given counsel that likewise is significant for us individually. First, the Lord provided Joseph with a needed sense of perspective, saying that "all these things" would be for "but a small moment" (D&C 121:7). Second, he made a humbling comparison, reassuring the suffering Prophet that he was "not yet as Job" (D&C 121:10). Along with this came the assurance that Joseph's enemies would ultimately fail as he finally would "triumph over all [his] foes" (see D&C 121:8, 11–22).

Furthermore, the adequacy of Joseph's remaining time in mortality was guaranteed and underscored: "Thy days are known, and thy years shall not be numbered less," because "there is a time appointed for every man, according as his works shall be" (D&C 122:9; 121:25). Joseph received no promise, however, of either immediate or total relief from adversity. Still more time was to be spent in Liberty Jail—along with persecutions and trials thereafter.

Concurrent with the reassurances, though then experiencing harsh abuses emanating from unrighteous political and military power, Joseph was given a starkly contrasting description of how God's power is to be exercised righteously (see D&C 121:34–46).

The foregoing counsel to the Prophet is for us likewise to heed in the midst of whatever we are called upon to endure. We need perspective as to the length of our trials; perspective as regards their comparative intensity; assurance that, if we are faithful, *our* enemies will not finally prevail, either; and assurance that life's timetable for us is likewise known to God, "according as [our] works shall be."

God said He would structure mortality to be a proving and testing experience (see Abraham 3:25; Mosiah 23:21). Clearly He has kept His promise and has carried out His divine intent. Therefore adversity must be part of the pattern rather than always an abberation. Therefore even our fiery trials, as Peter said, should not be thought of as being "some strange thing" (1 Peter 4:12). Hence throughout the varying lengths of our lives there is rolling relevance contained in the counsel to endure it well.

The challenges differ for each of us. Moreover, the configuration and weight of our own yoke of afflictions vary during the journey of discipleship such as in the differing seasons of our individual lives. Unvarying, however, is the reality that only by taking upon us the yoke Jesus assigns to us, and then enduring, will we learn most deeply of Him, love Him the more, and become more like Him (see Matthew 11:29).

Even though our yoke is tiny compared to His, the bearing process is the same. Still, some of us puzzle over the full meaning of the words, "For my yoke is easy, and my burden is light" (Matthew 11:30). True, as John wrote, "his commandments are not grievous" (1 John 5:3). Likewise, God is quick to bless us immediately in one way or another (see Mosiah 2:24). But the most profound relief waits to be claimed: our afflictions can be "swallowed up in the joy of Christ" (Alma 31:38). Only then the yoke and its burdens truly are eased.

There are many things we can be called upon to endure—such as illness, injustice, the insensitivity of others, poverty, the ironies of life, uncertainty, unpopularity, aloneness, unresponsiveness, being misrepresented and misunderstood, and sometimes seeing one-time friends not only draw away but actually become enemies. Paul reminded us that even the meek and lowly Jesus, though the Lord of the universe, nevertheless "endured . . . contradiction [opposition] of sinners against himself" (Hebrews 12:3).

Thus enduring well is clearly an essential part of mortality's planned refining process. Refining requires heat. Refining also requires time. Furthermore, if whatever constitutes "it" is to be endured well, refining also requires of its recipients a genuine and continuing confidence in the Refiner.

The painful and sometimes protracted process of refining is thus necessary in order to identify, separate, and cast off the dross. Uncharitableness, for instance, is to be burned away "in the furnace of affliction" (Isaiah 48:10; see also Alma 34:29). Our mortal tours in the "furnace of affliction" will vary widely as to frequency and intensity.

How could our personal empathy be genuinely and lastingly established and enlarged without refining experiences in the furnace of affliction? Even so, you and I do not loiter around these furnaces waiting for extra tours in those ovens.

Yet without enduring there could be no finishing or polishing.

It is not only the dross impurities that must go but also coarseness of all kinds. This is necessary in order for us to develop the highest forms of personality and character. In fact, the Greek word translated as *perfect* in Matthew 5:48 means "finished," "fully developed," or "complete." Therefore the dross is to be steadily removed in the refining process, while the precious cardinal qualities and attributes are to be etched everlastingly into one's soul.

While the process is most often gradual, Emily Dickinson noted the role that suddenness can sometimes play:

> He stuns you by degrees—
> Prepares your brittle Nature
> For the Ethereal Blow
> By fainter Hammers—further heard—
> Then nearer—Then so slow
> Your Breath has time to straighten—
> Your Brain—to bubble Cool—
> Deals—One—imperial—Thunderbolt—
> That scalps your naked Soul.[3]

Some defining and refining moments do seem to come upon us suddenly. Yet even what may seem to be sudden trials or defining moments may have been building in quiet crescendo for a long time. In any case there is no quick fix and no easy, mortal equivalent of the speedy microwave oven. Even if there were, would we be willing to trade the higher speed for the higher heat? The fiery trials are warm enough as it is. Besides, refining occurs gradually "in process of time."

It follows, then, that you and I cannot really expect to glide through life, coolly air-conditioned, while naively petitioning: "Lord, give me experience but not grief, a deeper appreciation of happiness but not deeper sorrow, joy in comfort but not in pain, more capacity to overcome but not more opposition; and please do not let me ever feel perplexed while on thine errand. Then let me come quickly and dwell with thee and fully share thy joy."

A further consideration is that in God's plan we mortals "are free to choose," among real alternatives (2 Nephi 2:27). In making these choices, as part of the test we face a vexing but necessary and built-in "opposition in all things" (2 Nephi 2:11). Inevitably many foolish and even wicked choices are made, causing a loving God to weep over His children's needless suffering (see Moses 7:28).

In furthering His plan for us, God seeks to tutor and to stretch us in order to refine us so that He can bring us home: "Nevertheless the Lord seeth fit to chasten his people; yea, he trieth their patience and their faith" (Mosiah 23:21). It is a process in which God has declared of His sobering but enhancing purposes for His children, "We will prove them herewith to see if they will do all things whatsoever the Lord their God shall command them" (Abraham 3:25).

The plan's developmental objective is clear: we are to "[put] off the natural man and become . . . a saint through the atonement of Christ the Lord, and become . . . as a child, submissive, meek, humble" (Mosiah 3:19).

We must not understand the words "to see if they will do" as suggesting that Heavenly Father did not already know, through His foreknowledge, whether individually and collectively we would do as He has commanded us. This is so for several reasons. First, given God's foreknowledge, He knows the outcomes beforehand. Second, the unfolding of a mortal experience with its trials is, in effect, a means of putting us clearly and incontestably on record as to the degree to which we have risen to meet the challenges of life. This open record is part of the justice of God, whose judgment and fairness will finally go uncontested (see Mosiah 16:1; 27:31; Alma 12:15).

Third, having passed through "all these things," we can thus see and know for ourselves whether or not we have risen to the challenges. If we succeed, we gain in confidence. If we do not, we ourselves will eventually understand and acknowledge that the failures were ours. Otherwise, how would we really know, for instance, that we are truly honest, or that we actually are spiritually submissive in a crunch, and so forth?

The Lord has carefully created this planet—our customized schoolhouse—in order that, being just the right distance from the sun, it would be environmentally inhabitable. Likewise, God has carefully designed the curriculum to be used therein so that it is strictly consistent with His proving purposes and our mortal agency. Walter Bagehot put it well:

If the universe were to be incessantly expressive and incessantly communicative, morality would be impossible: we should live under the unceasing pressure of a supernatural interference, which would give us selfish motives for doing everything, which would menace us with supernatural punishment if we left anything undone; we should be living in a *chastising* machine . . . the life which we lead and were meant to lead would be impossible . . . true virtue would become impossible. . . . A sun that shines and a rain which falls equally on the evil and on the good, are essential to morality in a being free like man and created as man was.[4]

There is a fourth and related reason. Though God already knows the outcomes, in order for us to grow as a result of the refining and the enduring that is to take place, nevertheless, we must actually pass through the experiences. There is no free admission to the "fellowship of his sufferings" (Philippians 3:10). Qualifying for the fellowship of his sufferings is something to be earned; it cannot be bestowed arbitrarily.

Whatever the individual details or sequence of the process, we need to endure a mix of trials. Some of these will be short and severe, others long and hard. Speaking of trials, Winston Churchill trenchantly observed that "we must learn to be equally good at what is short and sharp and what is long and tough."[5]

Divine tutorials, whether slow and stressful or sudden and harsh, call for us to ponder, again and again, the implications of this divine perspective: "The Son of Man hath descended below them all. Art thou greater than he?" (D&C 122:8.) As a result of His having "descended below all things," a magnificent outcome emerged "in that He comprehended all things" (D&C 88:6; see also 122:8). How essential His perfect empathy is to us imperfect mortals!

Stern tutorials can remind us of God's tender assurances and promises:

- My grace is sufficient for the meek (Ether 12:26).

- Fear not, little children, for you are mine, and I have overcome the world, and you are of them that my Father hath given me; (D&C 50:41).

- Wherefore, be of good cheer, and do not fear, for I the Lord am with you, and will stand by you; and ye shall bear record of me, even Jesus Christ, that I am the Son of the living God, that I was, that I am, and that I am to come (D&C 68:6).

- I . . . will be in [your] midst (D&C 32:3).

- Ye cannot bear all things now (D&C 50:40).

- Be of good cheer, for I will lead you along (D&C 78:18).

The Lord thus has His own ways of letting us know that He is with us in our individual furnaces of affliction, just as Shadrach, Meshach, and Abednego were not alone in their fiery furnace: "[There was] the form of the fourth . . . like the son of God" (Daniel 3:25).

It is not difficult to accept intellectually that the faithful who endure well a proximate deprivation now will receive the ultimate benefaction later: eternal life, the greatest of all the gifts of God (see D&C 14:7). But we are here. This is now. The trials are real. Temptations come daily. Can we learn to keep "all these things" in perspective?

Difficult as this can be, this is the course on which our faith must impel us if we are to endure it well. If we do not cling to this perspective, how can we expect to function fully and effectively in eternity without an acquired sense of proportion concerning which things matter most? Otherwise, in the context of a vast universe about which we know so little, how else will we have learned to be safe by being sufficiently submissive toward Him who knows all things? (See 2 Nephi 2:24; 9:20; D&C 130:7.) Otherwise, too, how will we have learned, firsthand, those eternal principles that, when obeyed, ensure everlasting happiness?

Without enduring the in-your-face, personal experiences in the here and now of this life, how useful will we be to Him in the there and then as He continues the "one eternal round" of His grand work and glory (see 1 Nephi 10:19; Moses 1:39)? Thus how could immortality be fully appreciated without an earned sense of proportion and perspective?

Clearly, the perspective particularly achieved by those who endure it well includes learning how to distinguish between what is big and what is small. The eminent historian Will Durant wrote of that human yearning for the perspective "to know that the little things are little, and the big things big, before it is too late; we want to see things now as they will seem forever—'in the light of eternity.' "6 Thus, without passing through mortality, how else will we learn to discern successfully what the "weightier matters of the law" really are (Matthew 23:23)? How else, too, will we get the practical and needed experience showing us that "the letter killeth, but the spirit giveth life" (2 Corinthians 3:6)?

Much refining needs to occur. Unless we endure it well, we will not have the right reflexes needed for the rest of eternity, reflexes we ourselves can trust completely and upon which others also can safely rely forever.

Without our individual refining, therefore, life would become merely a pass-through, audited course—not a course for credit. Only in the latter arrangement can our experiences and our performances be sanctified for our own everlasting good (see 2 Nephi 32:9). Mortality therefore is not a convenient, suburban, drive-around beltway with a view. Instead it passes slowly through life's inner city. Daily it involves real perspiration, real perplexity, real choosing, real suffering—and real refining!

Thus by its very nature the crucial process of refining cannot occur without our enduring. In what other way, pray tell, could our loving Father, who is so deeply committed to our moral agency and likewise to seeing us achieve greater happiness, possibly bring His purposes to pass?

There is no other way!

It is left to us, then, to learn the difference between the two as we grit our teeth rather than grind them destructively.

The refining and enduring process is of necessity painful and protracted. Moreover, the process requires our voluntary participation and our continued cooperation if it is to achieve any lasting results. Even Christ cannot perform our personal refining and enduring for us. He bore that huge, atoning portion—our sins—which we could not bear. Now He offers us His grace to help us endure our smaller portion, the painful refining process in which He separates the sin, which He hates, from His children, whom He loves.

"In process of time" the patina of pride is burnished off. Hearts that were so set on the things of the world, if sufficiently meek, will either go through "a mighty change" or be broken, so "a new heart" can be given (see D&C 121:35; Alma 5:14; Ezekiel 18:31; 36:26). The righteous and covenant-keeping individuals who endure it well will inherit "all that my Father hath" (D&C 84:38).

Ironically, often the most difficult part of enduring is choosing to begin the journey. We can pause too long as we contemplate this challenge or delay too long before we plunge into the process, causing too much needless trembling of the soul. It is vital therefore that we commence and then "continue as [we] commenced" (see D&C 9:5). Remember the story of the ancient crossing of the flood-swollen Jordan River (see Joshua 3:13–17). The Lord first required those who were carrying the ark of the covenant to step into the swollen river to get the soles of their feet wet, "dipped in the brim of the water." Only then did the Lord cause the river to "stand upon an heap," until all of the Israelites had passed over on dry ground. A willingness to get the soles of our feet wet is thus an important initiating step. This is the necessary starting point of the process of enduring and refining. After we so move, then the Lord moves!

> Until one is committed there is hesitancy, the chance to draw back, always ineffectiveness. Concerning all acts of initiative (and creation), there is one elementary truth, the ignorance of which kills countless ideas and splendid plans: that the moment one definitely commits oneself, then Providence moves too. All sorts of things occur to help one that would never otherwise have occurred. A whole stream of events issues from the decision, raising in one's favor all manner of unforeseen incidents and meetings and material assistance, which no man could have dreamt would have come his way.[7]

And there should be no turning back! Frustrated by a cancelled flight from Bombay to Karachi while en route on a tight timetable to meet with expectant Church members in Islamabad, Pakistan, I momentarily despaired. Lamenting with irritation to an airline official, I asked, "What are we supposed to do, go back to the hotel?" The official, more used to coping with airport chaos than I was, said, "Sir, you *never* go back to the hotel!"

After much perspiration and some inspiration, a substitute flight was found; the rendezvous with expectant members was kept. The official's words, however, are a metaphor for the trek of discipleship. "You *never* go back."

The words of Peter, Brigham Young, and in other scriptures, then, make clear that trials and adversities are not to be seen as a "strange thing" but are part of the normal pattern of life on earth. Mortality is a proving ground, a test of faith and obedience. By refining the submissive person, it makes him or her fit to return home to God. The course is not easy, but the grace of God is available to help us through it. And those who endure it well while clinging to the iron rod will receive the greatest of all gifts—eternal life.

From the time of Adam onward, Saints of all eras have faced this test in varying external conditions. For us today it is a discipleship to be achieved in a time when, as prophesied, "the whole earth shall be in commotion" (D&C 45:26).

2

FOLLOWING FIXED PRINCIPLES AMID COMMOTION

It was revealed to me in the commencement of this Church, that the Church would spread, prosper, grow and extend, and that in proportion to the spread of the Gospel among the nations of the earth, so would the power of Satan rise. (Brigham Young.)[1]

They are without principle, and past feeling (Moroni 9:20).

They are without principle," Moroni wrote. Without fixed principles and a clear destination, Nephi's metaphor of pressing forward amid "all these things" would give way to plodding persistence or mindless survival. But with gospel certitude his metaphor denotes a determined, zestful stride, even in those moments when there may seem to be nothing to be zestful about. Furthermore, in our day the striding forward "with a steadfastness in Christ" is to be accomplished amid the various expressions of how all things shall be in "commotion" in the world (see D&C 88:91; 2 Nephi 28:20). Much of this "commotion" may be geophysical, with earthquakes, seas heaving themselves beyond their bounds, and other such cataclysmic events. Disciples are also told, "When ye shall hear of wars and commotions, be not terrified; for these things must first come to pass; but the end is not by and by" (Luke 21:9; see also D&C 45:26; 88:91).

The Church therefore will "spread, prosper, grow and extend," but in a very challenging context, just as President Brigham Young foresaw. Yes, many things have yet to occur before Jesus' second coming, but God can cause events to be compressed. Once the fig trees have put forth their signalling leaves, such as "distress of nations, with perplexity," they do not retract them (see Matthew 24:32–33; Luke 21:25).

The informed chiliast, which a Latter-day Saint should be, is one who firmly believes in the literal second coming of Christ, which will usher in a millennial reign, but who can meet the special challenges involved in both noticing the leaves and enduring the heat of summer that follows. One is urged to notice, lest one be caught unawares. We may note merely two impressive indicators thus far: Has any age had more "signs and wonders" in the heavens than ours already has, with jet aircraft, manned and other satellites, and even journeys to the moon? Has any generation seen such ominous "vapours of smoke" as ours, with its atomic mushroom clouds over the pathetic pyres of Hiroshima and Nagasaki? (See D&C 45:41; Joel 2:30–31; Matthew 24:24; Acts 2:19.) But, alas, even these may fall short of later fulfillments.

Yet the careful observer must also be aware of how many false readings there have been in bygone times as well as in contemporary days, even by some of the faithful.

Our challenge in the days ahead, therefore, is one of balance, to notice the early warnings without overreacting and to move forward without slipping into the dulled heedlessness of the days of Noah (see Matthew 24:38–39). In those far distant days some doubtless jeered, or at least were privately amused, by the sight of Noah building his ark. Presumably, local mockery continued even when it began to rain torrentially and kept raining. But soon Noah's ark was the only safe and sane thing in a bewildering and desperate situation.

Thus we are to ponder signs without becoming paranoid, and to be aware without frantically keeping score between current events and scriptural expectations. The wise chiliast will use his or her energy in serving God and man instead of fretting and will resist secularism's heavy sedation.

Whatever the imminence of that great event, however, no serious student of the scriptures and no careful observer of the contemporary world will question how rigorous and trying our days already are—to say nothing of those that lie ahead when even more "things shall be in commotion" (D&C 88:91; see also Luke 21:9; D&C 45:26). In contrast to our turbulent times, William Manchester observed of life's comparative unchangingness as perceived in the Middle Ages: "In [ten centuries] nothing of real consequence had either improved or declined. Except for the introduction of waterwheels in the 800s and windmills in the late 1100s, there had been no inventions of significance. No startling new ideas had appeared, no new territories outside Europe had been explored. Everything was as it had been for as long as the oldest European could remember."[2]

As we look ahead, however, any toll that turbulence might take, amid the prophesied and dreaded events, might not bulk as large as the toll being steadily exacted on human hope by ongoing ethical relativism. Its effluence subtly saps much human hope and brings much subtle human misery. Ortega y Gasset said, regarding this spreading of relativism's fatal flaw: "If truth does not exist, relativism cannot take itself seriously. . . . Belief in truth is a deeply-rooted foundation of human life; if we remove it, life is converted into an illusion and an absurdity."[3]

Unanchored, society drifts, hardly able to cope with the illusory, with the irony, and with the absurdity, all of which form part of what was foreseen in terms of human commotion and the "distress of nations, with perplexity."

In the days that lie ahead things will not always go smoothly while we are building the kingdom. Usually individually but sometimes collectively, because of unforeseen circumstances, we may at times be held up in our journey, as it were, at a Winter Quarters. We may expect to move on sooner and cover more territory. There will be the equivalents of long, hard, hot days in crossing the plains of the secular wilderness. The best of our intentions will sometimes be countered by severe circumstances that may correspond in their call for heroism to those at Martin's Cove when our pioneer ancestors pressed forward anyway.

But despite the hardships there is a valley that lies ahead toward which we must move. Even after sadness and grief, as President Boyd K. Packer urged, we are to "pick up our handcarts and head west." That is a fixed principle, and without fixed principles and a steady spiritual focus for life we will be diverted by the cares of the world and intimidated by boldly striding secularism. It is very easy to underestimate the pervasiveness and preoccupations of secularism. Merely surviving, then striving for advantage, getting and spending; then being anesthetized by relentless routine, and sensing, as the secularist does, the finality of death—all these combine to ensure the grim dominance of the cares of the world.

It is likewise a grave error to underestimate secularism's dulling, desensitizing influence on traditional values. Jesus Himself compared the "business as usual" days of Noah and Lot with our own last days:

> And as it was in the days of Noe, so shall it be also in the days of the Son of man.
>
> They did eat, they drank, they married wives, they were given in marriage, until the day that Noe entered into the ark, and the flood came, and destroyed them all.
>
> Likewise also as it was in the days of Lot; they did eat, they drank, they bought, they sold, they planted, they builded;
>
> But the same day that Lot went out of Sodom it rained fire and brimstone from heaven, and destroyed them all.
>
> Even thus shall it be in the day when the Son of man is revealed. (Luke 17:26–30.)

Cataclysm came!

Two major symptoms of Noah's time were violence and corruption (see Genesis 6:11–12). Consider these depressing statistics regarding violence in today's United States:

> Only 7 percent of U.S. burglaries result in an arrest according to the National Center for Policy Analysis (NCPA). Of those arrested, 87 percent are prosecuted. Of those prosecuted, 79 percent are convicted. Of those convicted, a mere 25 percent are sent to prison. (Most are paroled.) After multiplying these probabilities, we see that a potential burglar faces only a 1.2 percent chance of going to prison for each act of burglary committed. Once in prison, he will stay there for about 13 months. But since he will escape imprisonment more than 98 percent of the time, the expected "cost" of each burglary to the burglar is only 4.8 days.[4]

How does one proceed with living and enduring well in such a world? How can we develop and maintain "a perfect brightness of hope" in a period of prophesied "gloominess"? (See Joel 2:2.) It helps to face squarely some of the underlying causes of the "gloominess" in which we live.

Solving society's problems is made much more difficult because of the failure to correctly diagnose their causes. Discerning between possible solutions and treating mere symptoms becomes much more difficult without gospel fulness. Without utilizing fixed principles, confused mortals will find things very hard to fix.

Without truth-trained perspective, some individuals will overreact to some supposed or short-term human successes, as did economist and free trader Richard Cobden, who in 1846 gushed that the repeal of Britain's Corn Laws was "the most important event in history since the coming of Christ." As important as that legislation may have been to some back then, clearly Cobden was carried away—and not by the Spirit!

If we do not acknowledge God and His ordering principles we will end up walking stubbornly in our own ways, thus producing the worst form of inflation and the hardest to cure: inflated egos.

On TV we see dramas that hype immorality and dishonor chastity and marital fidelity, along with occasional specials on the serious problem of children born out of wedlock and on the break-up of the family. Such inconsistency reflects a lack of fundamental integrity. Similarly, humanistic morality—"I hope I can forgive myself"—also abounds; its insularity contains no remedy and is completely unlike the meekly inquiring Apostles in their asking Jesus, "Lord, is it I?" (Matthew 26:22.) Ethical relativism eases the coasting down the adversary's carefully prepared slope (see 2 Nephi 28:21).

Superficially saying "I am sorry" is a popular mantra, but it guarantees no real change, either. There is so much shouted justification and so little quiet shame! Others may feel justified in saying "I have done nothing wrong," because with ethical relativism wrong is virtually defined "out of existence." Moreover, sorrowful sentimentality cannot cleanse us. Rather, it merely adds to mortal despair and distress.

If there is no acknowledgment of divine standards, justice and mercy become vague and fuzzy concepts instead of powerful principles. In that situation, even though some of them have caused gross suffering, sympathy is lavished on the guilty even before there is any consideration of justice and real repentance.

No wonder we also see a loss of righteous indignation. There is plenty of indignation all right, but most often it represents selfish egos, not righteous principles. Nowadays people are so much more easily offended, while being much less concerned about offending God.

No wonder too that we see so much "sorrowing of the damned"—this by those in a psychological no-man's-land (see Mormon 2:12–13). These individuals can no longer take pleasure in sin, but they do not fully repent, either. They hope somehow to be saved *in* their sins instead of being willing to "give away all [their] sins" in order to know God (Alma 22:18).

All about us we see hypocrisies as between public and private behavior, as if God had issued two sets of commandments—one for indoors and another for out-of-doors.

This means that humans desperately need correct views of our true identity and of God's purposes for us, His children. Likewise they desperately need to be reassured of the existence of an immortal but also kind God, as was Enoch: "yet thou art there" (Moses 7:30). Enoch went on to testify not only of the reality of the existence of our Father but, further, that He is "just, . . . merciful and kind forever" (Moses 7:30). It is not only an awareness of God that draws us to Him but also what He is like. Do we not sing: "We doubt not the Lord nor his goodness. We've proved Him in days that are past"?5

Going home to Him cannot happen except we are able to "see things as they really are" and "things as they really will be" (Jacob 4:13), so that amid the challenges of life we can better endure it well by having gospel perspectives. Otherwise we can be so easily preoccupied with or diverted by lesser things.

The Lord told the Prophet in 1831, "Ye hear of wars in far countries, and you say that there will soon be great wars in far countries, but ye know not the hearts of men in your own land" (D&C 38:29; see also D&C 87:1). In our time we don't understand fully the hearts of some of our countrymen, either. Nor do many see fully the implications of social fragmentation and the diminution of the family. It is all made even worse because of evils and designs in the hearts of conspiring men in the last days—and not just those pertaining to the tycoons of tobacco and alcohol (see D&C 89:4).

Evil, designing, and conspiring individuals understand very well how easy it is to titillate and ensnare the natural man. Why, therefore, do so many applaud, such as for their advertising cleverness, people who parade alcoholic temptations before an alcoholic? There is a significant difference between being genuinely "sorry" for an individual who shoots himself in the foot and applauding him for so doing. The sharp, fundamental differences between worldly sorrow and godly sorrow become apparent, again and again (see 2 Corinthians 7:10).

When society casts aside the traditional Judeo-Christian values, therefore, watch the tendency to give more attention to perpetrators than to their victims. The foregoing errancies are merely indicative of what is to be endured by the faithful.

God described to Enoch the essential causes of the vast and needless human suffering: "And unto thy brethren have I said, and also given commandment, that *they should love one another*, and that *they should choose me*, their Father; *but* behold, *they are without affection*, and *they hate their own blood*" (Moses 7:33, emphasis added).

The prophet Moroni recorded the clear consequences of what happened when his people became grossly desensitized: "They have lost their love, one towards another; and they thirst after blood and revenge continually . . . [they are] without civilization . . . delight . . . in so much abomination. . . . without order and without mercy. . . . strong in their perversion. . . . without principle, and past feeling." (See Moroni 9:5–20.)

Likewise, once we begin to walk in our own preoccupied ways, even if they are reasonably decent, we tend to "pass by" people who are in need and "notice them not" (Mormon 8:39).

Decrease the belief in God, therefore, and behold the large increase in the numbers of those who wish to play at being God. Such societal supervisors may deny the existence of divine ways but they are very serious about imposing their own ways.

Those who disavow the existence of absolute truths must forego the disapproving of anything on moral grounds. They may try to evoke a response by using all the old words, but these went out of fashion with the old values. Words minus their moral content cannot for long be meaningfully appropriated.

Once a society loses its capacity to declare that some things are wrong *per se*, it finds itself forever building temporary defenses, drawing new lines but forever falling back and losing its nerve. A society which permits simply anything will eventually lose everything!

The family of man is in deep trouble, in large measure because the institution of the family, at least in much of the western world, is in deep trouble. This situation and other indicators so tell us, if we have eyes to see.

As the Church spreads across the earth, so does Satan's dominion. Prophesied for our day are such things as wars, commotions,
and distress of nations. These are not all geophysical. Perhaps even
more destructive is the ethical relativism that denies any spiritual
order and rejects divine and fixed principles of right and wrong.
This we see reflected in a wholesale decline in moral standards and
in the rapidly escalating incidence of cruelty, crime, and corruption.

Latter-day Saints, however, recognize the need for and adhere
to fixed principles that have a clear and positive destination in view.
This requires that we press forward consistently in righteous
efforts that will bring us to that goal.

3

PRESSING FORWARD IN THE DAYS AHEAD

Do not let us speak of darker days; let us speak rather of sterner days. These are not dark days: these are great days— the greatest days our country has ever lived; and we must all thank God that we have been allowed, each of us according to our stations, to play a part in making these days memorable in the history of our race. (Winston Churchill.)[1]

Is our society beyond the point of return? One lesson of Nineveh is that we must not give up. But episodic and loose confederacies of decent people will be no match for the evils and designs of conspiring people, for "behold, the enemy is combined" (D&C 38:12). This warning is to be taken seriously both individually and collectively. "Wherefore let him that thinketh he standeth take heed lest he fall" (1 Corinthians 10:12).

So it is, therefore, that more than any preceding generation in the Church, we—and especially the rising generations—are destined to serve in a period of human history which will be "stern" indeed.

What follows below by way of indicators is representative of those circumstances we are told to endure well. (The charts reflect the United States situation and are based on research done by Perry Cunningham and Kristen Goodman for a CES satellite broadcast talk I gave on 4 June 1995.) Some recitation and contemplation of these trends is part of our preparation in order that we may "overcome the world" in our days. Since the "enemy is combined," it is well to assess the patterns and consequences of his order of battle, how his forces are deployed, and what objectives he seeks. Scanning and pondering key symptoms can thus be a help.

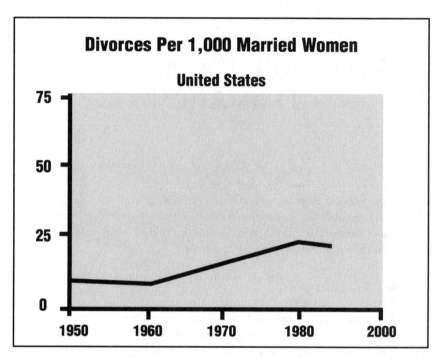

1. *Divorce.* If current divorce levels persist, about 50 percent of all marriages contracted in the past fifteen to twenty years will end in divorce. Of all marriages contracted in 1995, it is expected that 60 percent will end in divorce. Half of the children whose parents divorce and remarry will also experience a second such family disruption before they reach age sixteen.

In the 1960s, only 7 percent of college students came from homes where the parents were divorced. By the early 1990s, that number had risen to over 30 percent!

Bruce Hafen, Provost at Brigham Young University and Professor of Law, in his extensive studies covering "Marriage and the State's Legal Posture Toward the Family," has written that "American law has taken the freedom to obtain a divorce further than the law of any Western nation." He cites Harvard Law Professor Mary Ann Glendon that "in the last generation American society has experienced a 'transformation' in its laws and in its views on family life that is 'the most fundamental shift [in the state's legal posture toward the family] since the Protestant Reformation.' "2 This disturbing development is part of the foreseen "commotion."

In the same address to the American Bar Association, Provost Hafen included two biting questions that bear upon the signs of our times:

> As social scientists Elshrain and Popenoe put it, "The most important causal factor of declining child well-being is the remarkable collapse of marriage, leading to growing family instability and decreasing parental investment in children."
>
> [The] evidence now overwhelmingly confirms G.K. Chesterton's remark that we should "regard a system that produces many divorces as we do a system that drives men to drown or shoot themselves."3

2. *Single-parent families.* In 1960, 73 percent of the nation's children lived with two natural parents who were married only once. Of the children born in 1986, however, 60 percent will spend a portion of their childhood in a one-parent situation.

3. *Employed mothers of preschoolers.* Today, many single mothers

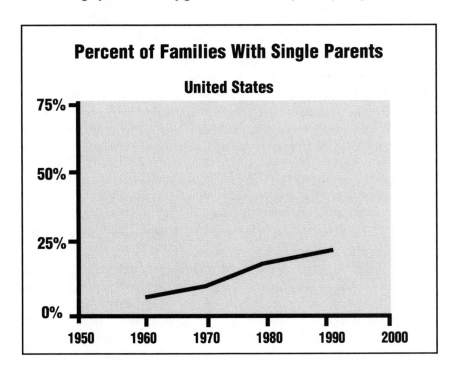

work out of sheer necessity; some valiantly try to keep their families intact. Yet we are compelled to consider that back in 1950 only 12 percent of the mothers with preschool children were in the labor force. By 1993, it was 60 percent!

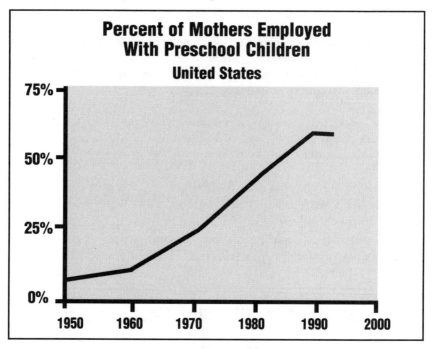

Percent of Mothers Employed With Preschool Children

United States

4. *Illegitimate births.* In 1950, 13 percent of the births to fifteen-to nineteen-year-olds were to unmarried women. By 1990, it was 67 percent! Looking ahead from 1995, the overall national illegitimacy rate "is predicted to reach 50 percent within the next twelve to twenty years."[4]

This last trend is not only ominous, it is unprecedented! Gertrude Himmelfarb has warned: "The present illegitimacy ratio is not only unprecedented in the past two centuries; it is unprecedented, so far as we know, in American history going back to colonial times, and in English history from Tudor times."[5]

5. *Children not living with their biological fathers.* About 40 percent of U.S. children now sleep in homes without a resident father. Presently, more than half of the American children will spend a portion of their childhood living apart from their fathers. It may soon rise to 60 percent.

Consider but one consequence of how lamentable this trend

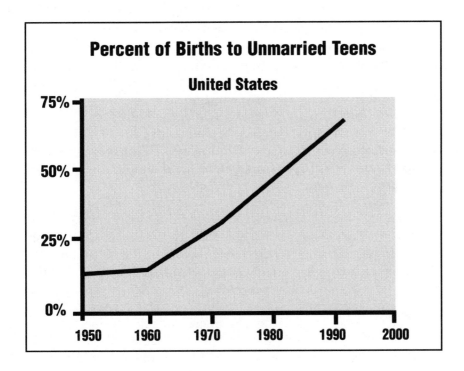

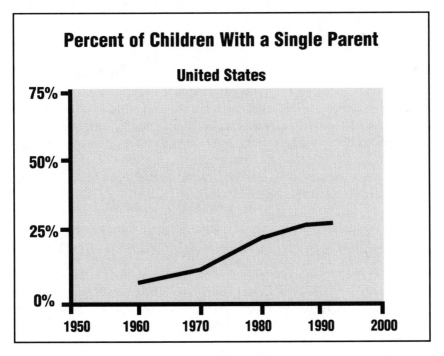

is: More than 70 percent of all juveniles in state reform institutions come from fatherless homes. There is a bitter harvest largely as a result of so much breaking of the seventh commandment.

Today, therefore, we have more functioning gadgets of convenience but fewer functioning fathers! Consider how needless divorce sends a scorching signal to children about how unimportant they are, as does the message adult live-ins send to teens about the acceptability of sexual immorality. What are sons raised in fatherless homes supposed to understand about either the role of fathers or the importance of families?

It is not surprising, therefore, that so many interconnections between people and also between people and institutions are fraying. This is more of the prophesied commotion. One writer observed that there is "an inevitable fraying of the net of connections between people at many critical intersections, of which the marital knot is only one. Each fraying accelerates others. A break in one connection, such as attachment to a stable community, puts pressure on other connections: marriage, the relationship between parents and children, religious affiliation, a feeling of connection with the past—even citizenship, that sense of membership in a large community which grows best when it is grounded in membership in a small one."[6]

The several destructive trends just cited cannot be reversed with a snap of society's fingers. In fact, if we hear any snaps they will be the sounds of more fraying among the vital interconnections.

Many things will not get better until and unless we have better, stronger families. But this will require much more self-denial, and, ironically, self-denial is a quality best developed in loving families. Hence the fact that current problems were foreseen did nothing to stay their advance. In 1965, Sen. Daniel Patrick Moynihan, D-N.Y., then assistant secretary of labor, issued a warning:

> A community that allows a large number of young men to grow up in broken homes, dominated by women, never acquiring any stable relationship to male authority, never acquiring any rational expectations about the future—that community asks for and gets chaos. . . . (In such a society) crime, violence, unrest, unrestrained lashing out at the whole social structure—these are not only to be expected, they are virtually inevitable.[7]

It is more than a coincidence that each of these trends, which devastate the family, accelerated during the same time period! Furthermore, it is not only today's America that is in trouble. So are the next generations, who will live dangerously "downwind" from these contaminating conditions.

These anti-family trend lines are like a several-headed Hydra, each with its own venom of consequences.

A related consideration pertains to advocacy in behalf of families: "The truth is that only men to whom the family is sacred will ever have a standard or a status by which to criticize the state. They alone can appeal to something more holy than the gods of the city; the gods of the hearth."[8]

Like the subtle serpent spoken of biblically, this Hydra surely and steadily bruises mankind (see Genesis 3:1, 12–15). Even so, as far as our individual lives are concerned, its influence can at least be contained by our personal righteousness.

It is worthy of note that warning voices are not confined to religious sources. Other forecasts are becoming increasingly foreboding, including one warning that "any further reduction—either in functions or in number of [family] members—will likely

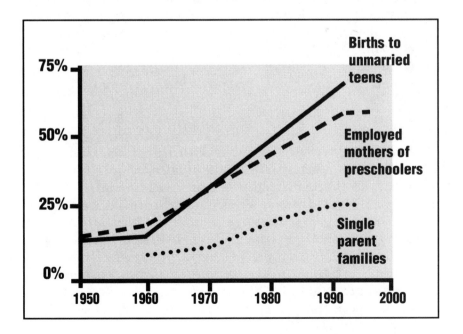

have adverse consequences for children, and thus for generations to come."9

As if this pattern, by itself, were not alarming enough, these "worst of times" trends are also undercutting of the "best of times" advantages.

There is more education, but there is less hope. Paul Rogat Loeb quotes Christopher Lasch in his observation that if our young have no hope for the future, this is in great part because we have left them ignorant of their past: "If young people feel no connection to anything, . . . their dislocation is a measure of our failure, not theirs. We have failed to provide them with a culture that claims to explain the world or [that] links the experience of one generation to those that came before and to those that will follow."10

This life's temporal lens distorts. The things of the moment are grossly magnified, and the things of eternity are blurred or diminished. No wonder God asks us mortals to trust His perfect love and His perfect knowledge!

There is generally better health, but various plagues will come (see D&C 84:97; 87:6; Revelation 21:9).

There is more personal mobility but much, much less community.

There are more and better highways, but fewer safe streets. Since 1960, violent crime in America is up 560 percent!

The knowledge explosion is certainly real, but with it there is a disconnecting and trivialization of some truths. This is occurring amid a flood of information. Neil Postman argues effectively that the connection between information and human purpose has been severed.11

So many, therefore, are "ever learning, and never able to come to the knowledge of the truth" (2 Timothy 3:7). No wonder T. S. Eliot lamented, "Where is the wisdom we have lost in knowledge? Where is the knowledge we have lost in information?"12

Way back when these trends had barely started, prophetic voices were raised. For one, President Stephen L Richards spoke in 1958 of the urgent need to put an exemplary "father back at the head of the family." President Richards saw fathers beginning to distance themselves from their families, but he also foresaw "an ever-increasing calamity that shakes our very national life, not only for present generations but that may shape its course for ages to come."13 The foreseen "calamity" is upon us, and it is shaking "our very national life."

But the public was not in a listening mood back then. Political and educational leaders did not then see or care to see the gathering storm. Many were not only imperceptive but also smug. Their smugness reminds one of the attitude of "that ancient retiree from the Research Department of the British Foreign Office [who] reportedly said, after serving from 1903 to 1950: 'Year after year the worriers and fretters would come to me with awful predictions of the outbreak of war. I denied it each time. I was wrong only twice.' [World War I and World War II.]"[14]

As we strive to "endure well" the macro, societal, and global challenges which form the context of our days, it is comforting to know that we are not left alone, for our God is a personal God. Note the following customized, divine communications:

"And the night following the Lord stood by him, and said, Be of good cheer, Paul: for as thou hast testified of me in Jerusalem, so must thou bear witness also at Rome" (Acts 23:11). The resurrected Lord of the universe visited one person in a castle jail: He extended appreciation to Paul. He gave him encouragement, and He also gave him a "missionary transfer" from Jerusalem to Rome. How big was Jesus' audience? One!

Jesus was likewise disclosing and encouraging to a believing, solitary woman of Samaria, another audience of one, to whom, by the way, He disclosed "all that ever [she] did" (see John 4:39). "The woman saith unto him, I know that Messias cometh, which is called Christ: when he is come, he will tell us all things. Jesus saith unto her, I that speak unto thee am he." (John 4:25–26.)

Thus the Lord of the universe, early in His ministry, disclosed His true identity to an audience of one. He knows each and all of us, too. And as in the instance of the woman of Samaria, He knows all things we have ever done, and He knows what lies ahead of us. And He loves us. He can steady us individually even in the midst of general commotion.

The Prophet Joseph and the revelations confirm that God lives in an "eternal now," where the past, present, and future are continually before Him. He is not constrained by the perspectives of time as are we. He sees the end from the beginning. You and I, on the other hand, are in the muddled, mortal middle. So when we are discouraged, let us keep in mind the Prophet Joseph's assurance that God has made "ample provision" in order to accomplish His purposes even in the midst of human wickedness.[15] His plan has taken things into account beforehand. In this manner and with such faith we can live comforted and assured in the midst of challenges, including the devastating trends that will increasingly beset the times in which we live.

We are involved in an unfolding which we can only see through a glass darkly, but which the Lord sees with the unique clarity of omniscience. For instance, President Brigham Young observed of certain political disorders and upheavals in the world with their attendant miseries and difficulties, that, even so, out of these there could come some benefit, because in those nations "the door will be opened and the gospel will be preached to all."[16]

Nephi said he once heard the voice of the Father. Among all He might have said, what did the Father choose to say in one of those special moments? He declared that the words of His Son were true, but He also emphasized how important it is that we *endure to the end* (see 2 Nephi 31:15). Nephi beautifully associated the capacity to endure with pressing forward, feasting on the scriptures, and developing the capacity to love (2 Nephi 31:20). So positioned, we will be able to deflect the fiery darts of the adversary or quench them with the shield of faith. After all, Jesus has forewarned us of these times: "Behold, I speak these things unto you for the elect's sake; and you also shall hear of wars, and rumors of wars; see that ye be not troubled, for all I have told you must come to pass; but the end is not yet. Behold, I have told you before." (Joseph Smith–Matthew 1:23–24.)

It is a marvelous thing to see how the gospel enlightens us and tames us. Sin does just the opposite; it dulls, darkens, and hardens us. One ongoing miracle in the Church is people whose faith is sufficiently strong that they are letting the gospel tame and remodel them.

These really are our days, and we can prevail and overcome, even in the midst of trends that are very disturbing. If we are faithful the day will come when those deserving pioneers and ancestors, whom we rightly praise for having overcome the adversities in their wilderness trek, will praise today's faithful for having made their way successfully through a desert of despair and for having passed through a cultural wilderness, while still keeping the faith.

We can make of these days ahead "days never to be forgotten" in the history of the Church. Ours can be "a voice of gladness" even amid the stern but foreseen days of "gloominess," while being "alive in Christ" in the living Church. (See Joseph Smith–History 1, footnote to verse 71; D&C 128:19; 2 Nephi 25:25.)

4

PURSUING DISCIPLESHIP IN A LIVING CHURCH

You all know that it takes intelligence to enjoy. . . . I say, if you want to enjoy exquisitely, become a Latter-day Saint, and then live the doctrine of Jesus Christ. (Brigham Young.)[1]

The restored Church of Jesus Christ is vital in assisting us to achieve exaltation and greatly aids us as we strive to grow and to endure and to enlarge our capacity for true joy.

President Brigham Young, while testifying of the restored and living Church, gave this practical caution: "This is the kingdom that was to be set up in the last days. It is like a stone taken from the mountain without hands, with all its roughness, with all its disfigured appearance—uncomely—even a stumbling-block and a stone of offence to the nations of the earth."[2]

We are, in fact, a part of what at least in some respects is regarded in the eyes of the world as a "strange work," "disfigured" and "uncomely" (see Isaiah 28:21). No wonder some are so dismissive of the Church, as they seek to explain it away or to push it away!

As we consider the context in which we live, including various and vexing trends, it is ever to be borne in mind that the Church is surely not trendy, though too many of its members, alas, follow the trends of the world.

The Lord, perceiving in advance these human prejudices, described His restored work as a "strange act" and "strange work" being brought to pass, so that some men might get over their stumbling blocks and ponder "that which they have never considered" (D&C 101:94, 95; 95:4; Isaiah 28:21).

A major stumbling block of the Jews in Jesus' day, for instance, was their expectation about what the Messiah would do when He came, such as emancipating them politically. But Jesus of Nazareth was not such an emancipator; thus to the Jews His death was a confirming stumbling block! This irony had been prophesied (see Psalm 118:22; Isaiah 8:14; John 1:5). The Greeks, on the other hand, regarded the whole idea of a crucified Messiah as foolishness (see 1 Corinthians 1:23). The day will come, however, when there will be a "taking away of their stumbling blocks" (1 Nephi 14:1).

A fresh view of things is thus not always welcomed. What can seem to be a strange perspective can actually be jarring to those intensely set in their ways (see Psalm 118:22). Even the remarkable Enoch was not welcomed by many of his contemporaries. Of him and his labors it was said, "There is a strange thing in the land" (Moses 6:38).

Nevertheless, in a time of prophesied perplexity, enhanced knowledge and perspective concerning the living God and Jesus is vital, and this richness came with the Restoration. Brigham Young observed perceptively: "The Lord is kind to this people, and if we could understand *things as they really are* and be as willing to help ourselves as the Lord is to help us, we should advance much more rapidly in the knowledge of God than we do"[3] (see Jacob 4:13).

The living Church is the recipient and the repository of continuing and much-needed revelation, including additional scriptures. The Church is the preserver and sharer of divine doctrines, as it administers all the legal ordinances and covenants essential to salvation and exaltation, including those to be discussed in this chapter. Each of these provisions in man's behalf is also vital to helping us "endure it well."

The living Church, led by the living God through living prophets, counsels, directs, and at times even reproves its members, thus helping us *to do* and *to be* that which is needed for admission to the upper realms of God's celestial kingdom, the ultimate and complete homecoming.

Certain non-waiveable things are essential, however, in order for us to obtain eternal life. These things include what we are *to do* and what we are *to be*. Sometimes we give too little thought to what we are *to be*. Yet Jesus clearly asks us to become "even as I am," calling attention to "the weightier matters" such as judgment, mercy, and faith (see Matthew 5:48; 3 Nephi 12:48; 3 Nephi 27:27; Matthew 23:23).

In order to enter the kingdom of heaven we must be childlike. This term describes a particular manner of men and women (see Matthew 18:3; 2 Peter 1:4–7; 3:11). But what do those requirements mean? King Benjamin spells out the angel's message in his marvelous sermon, describing how, through Jesus' atonement, one can "[become] a saint . . . as a child, submissive, meek, humble, patient, full of love, willing to submit to all things which the Lord seeth fit to inflict upon him, even as a child doth submit to his father" (Mosiah 3:19).

Striving to incorporate these cardinal qualities makes us more saintly and helps us immeasurably to endure it well. Significantly, submissiveness, that reverent expression of enduring, is mentioned twice. Giving enduring extra emphasis is capped by directing that we "submit to" and endure "all things which the Lord seeth fit to inflict upon [us], even as a child doth submit to his father" (Mosiah 3:19). Much of enduring well requires this reverent submissiveness. The living Church greatly facilitates living discipleship in which opportunities and reminders of the needed virtues are all about us.

Developing these saintly qualities is every bit as essential as receiving the ordinances of the gospel. Even the gifts of God are not of full use if one has not, for instance, developed the quality of charity:

> Though I speak with the tongues of men and of angels, and have not charity, I am become as sounding brass, or a tinkling cymbal.
>
> And though I have the gift of prophecy, and understand all mysteries, and all knowledge; and though I have all faith, so that I could remove mountains, and have not charity, I am nothing.
>
> And though I bestow all my goods to feed the poor, and though I give my body to be burned, and have not charity, it profiteth me nothing. (1 Corinthians 13:1–3.)

Thus developing charity is clearly just as essential for admission to the upper realms of the celestial kingdom as is baptism! We are to be more than merely nice; rather, we are to be "full of love" (Mosiah 3:19). Moroni could not have been more declarative on this point: "And now I know that this love which thou hast had for the children of men is charity; wherefore, except men shall have charity they cannot inherit that place which thou hast prepared in the mansions of thy Father." (Ether 12:34.)

It is significant that all the cardinal virtues flow from charity—patience, submissiveness, mercy, and so forth. "There is one virtue, attribute, or principle, which, if cherished and practiced by the Saints, would prove salvation to thousands upon thousands. I allude to charity, or love, from which proceed forgiveness, long-suffering, kindness, and patience."[4]

Charity thus initiates and sustains all spiritual qualities. Sometimes the discussions in the Church regarding the nature and extent of God's love occur in reaction to the positions of others. Those, for instance, who feel God's love is unconditional—as if somehow his caring for us made Him uncaring about our sins—see themselves moving to the "starboard side" in order to balance those who feel God's love is severely conditional, and vice versa.

God loves all His spirit children. How could it be otherwise, since He is a perfect Father? In that sense His love is universal and everlasting for all of His children. But He does not and cannot love our wickedness: "For I the Lord cannot look upon sin with the least degree of allowance" (D&C 1:31). He does not and cannot approve of the things we do that are wrong, nor will He say on Judgment Day, "Well done, thou good and faithful servant" to those who have been wicked or who have been poor performers. His perfect integrity and His perfected attributes of truth and justice would not permit it. Nor can our Heavenly Father reward us evenly, because our deeds and our degrees of righteousness are so very uneven. Of necessity, therefore, we are told there are "many mansions" in His house, and only of the comparative few can it be said, "all that my Father hath shall be given" (John 14:2; D&C 84:38). It is especially of such faithful that Paul writes: "Who shall separate us from the love of Christ? shall tribulation, or distress, or persecution, or famine, or nakedness, or peril, or sword? . . . Nor height, nor depth, nor any other creature, shall be able to separate us from the love of God, which is in Christ Jesus our Lord." (Romans 8:35, 39.)

It is because God loves us, however, that He seeks with such vigor and long-suffering to separate us from our sins, which He hates. He continues to care for us even when He cannot approve of us. Yet ultimately we cannot go where He is unless He fully approves of us. This outcome, however, reflects the consequences of divine justice, not His love for us, which persists.

Likewise it is because He loves us that His redemptive arm "is lengthened out all the day long" (2 Nephi 28:32). Yet even after all of His outreaching and loving long-suffering, there will follow the judgment and justice of God. Thus His long-suffering is not indulgence masquerading as mercy.

God will never stop loving all of His spirit children, including those who go to the telestial kingdom, a kingdom of glory which, because of God's generosity, "surpasses all understanding" (D&C 76:89).

Thus the hard, cold fact is that how we use our moral agency does not result in a withdrawal of God's love but does determine the ways and the degrees to which a loving God can express His love of us. Only the most righteous will receive His praise, His approval, and enjoy His presence. These supernal blessings are conditionally bestowed. However, as a perfect Father He loves all of His spirit children! The more we understand His character and His love, the more poignant is any separation from Him.

It is *our* love of *Him* that needs to be proven. If we are unrighteous, "the Spirit of the Lord is grieved" (D&C 121:37). He is "grieved" precisely because He loves us so deeply. But do we love Him enough to set things right in our lives? This is the continuing test.

The large attributes, those that cover the most ground, are almost always developed incrementally—by small steps, small decisions, and small initiatives. The attributes and talents we bring with us from the premortal world were most likely developed there in the same way. Yet upon seeing someone with highly developed cardinal attributes we may respond that "he was born that way." Whatever the case, so far as the mortal life is concerned it is what we do with these qualities that matters.

Imagine, for instance, the differing outcomes if Abraham Lincoln had been less able to endure personal and political tragedy. Douglas Southall Freeman wrote eloquently of Lincoln:

> Had Lincoln died in a cabin, men would not have thought it remarkable that he had been born in one. Had he not mauled Stephen A.

Douglas, they would not have reminded the world that he had mauled rails. The manger grows in significance only as we approach the open tomb. . . .

When Lincoln came to Washington, the clouds had never been so dark and the danger so acute. And to the despairing, it seemed that during the whole history of the Union never had there come to the presidential chair a man less adequately equipped than was this stranger from Illinois. . . .

But Lincoln was ready. The stream of his strength was flowing full-banked. It had passed the meadows of doubt. It was flooded with high purpose, and soon it was to be joined with that other stream to make his self-mastery complete—the conquest of his own spirit. . . .

This full self-mastery of Lincoln you will find in that patient fixity of purpose that characterized every movement in the deep stream of his stalwart soul. . . . And well it was that he had learned not to weary of the battle! For when he came to Washington, he found himself opposed not merely by gallant armies, most brilliantly led, but badgered and opposed, misunderstood and maligned by men of his own nation and often of his own party.[5]

Suppose similarly that George Washington had possessed less integrity and meekness. What then would have happened in the founding of the United States? Rich personal qualities have their consequences—public and private, personal and national. Deficiencies have their real consequences, too. Of course, our weaknesses are sometimes a spur. People strongly driven by ego may accomplish things that otherwise might have gone undone. Thus it is likewise marvelous to see how the Lord can use us even with our deficiencies.

The point, therefore, is not to be picky-picky or ungrateful concerning the contributions of outstanding men and women who have made special contributions in spite of some large, personal weaknesses, for we "all . . . come short of the glory of God" (Romans 3:23). Whatever the varied contributions off such individuals, however, these did not cancel their need to control their excesses.

God wishes to share His glory more fully with us but can only do so based on eternal, nonarbitrary rules. These terms include our striving to become more like Him (see Matthew 5:48; 3 Nephi 12:48; 27:27). Thus, even now, the better we are, the better it is for all whose lives we touch.

But let us note the things we are *to do* and *to receive*, for these greatly facilitate enduring. The things we are to do and to receive are likewise nonnegotiable, nonwaiveable requirements for entering into the presence of God. Alas, for many mortals these things seem to be antique and even quaint requirements. As we have come to know by means of the restored gospel of Jesus Christ, however, these things are essential, just as the sample scriptures that follow illustrate and confirm.

Faith in the Lord is essential, as these scriptures clearly indicate, not only to qualify for the celestial kingdom but also to succeed in life itself.

The valiant in the celestial kingdom will be those "who received the testimony of Jesus, and believed on his name" and "who overcome by faith, and are sealed by the Holy Spirit of promise, which the Father sheds forth upon all those who are just and true" (D&C 76:51, 53). Thus, "without faith it is impossible to please him: for he that cometh to God must believe that he is, and that he is a rewarder of them that diligently seek him" (Hebrews 11:6).

Faith is essential not only for salvation but also for successful daily life. "For we walk by faith, not by sight" (2 Corinthians 5:7).

Faith stirs us to *repentance,* which is an equally essential requirement: "all men, everywhere, must repent, or they can in nowise inherit the kingdom of God, for no unclean thing can dwell there, or dwell in his presence" (Moses 6:57); "begin to exercise your faith unto repentance . . . that [God] would have mercy upon you" (Alma 34:17); "and the time is at hand that [the unrepentant] must repent or he cannot be saved" (Alma 5:31).

Baptism and *receiving the Holy Ghost* are nonnegotiable requirements, too:

> Jesus answered, Verily, verily, I say unto thee, Except a man be born of water and of the Spirit, he cannot enter into the kingdom of God (John 3:5).

> For the gate by which ye should enter is repentance and baptism by water; and then cometh a remission of your sins by fire and by the Holy Ghost (2 Nephi 31:17).

> Ye must be born again into the kingdom of heaven, of water, and

of the Spirit, and be cleansed by blood, even the blood of mine Only Begotten; that ye might be sanctified from all sin, and enjoy the words of eternal life in this world, and eternal life in the world to come, even immortal glory (Moses 6:59).

Note that baptism and the Holy Ghost permit us to "enjoy the words of eternal life in this world." In the absence of these two prerequisites, however, individuals will not really "enjoy" the holy scriptures or the words of the living prophets. This is no small clue as to why some are put off by, rather than become attached to, the Church and the gospel.

The Melchizedek Priesthood is essential for eternal life. Men hold that holy priesthood and women share fully in its blessings.

> And this greater priesthood administereth the gospel and holdeth the key of the mysteries of the kingdom, even the key of the knowledge of God. . . .
>
> And without the ordinances thereof, and the authority of the priesthood, the power of godliness is not manifest unto men in the flesh;
>
> For without this no man can see the face of God, even the Father, and live. (D&C 84:19, 21–22.)

> Therefore, all those who receive the priesthood, receive this oath and covenant of my Father, which he cannot break, neither can it be moved (D&C 84:40).

All temple blessings, ordinances, and covenants are likewise essential:

> Therefore, . . . your anointings, and your washings, and your baptisms for the dead, . . . are ordained by the ordinance of my holy house, which my people are always commanded to build unto my holy name (D&C 124:39).

> . . . in the which house I design to endow those whom I have chosen with power from on high (D&C 95:8).

> . . . it is expedient in me that the first elders of my church should receive their endowment from on high in my house (D&C 105:33).

Being *sealed* is, therefore, clearly essential to eternal life: "In the celestial glory there are three heavens or degrees; and in order to obtain the highest, a man must enter into this order of the priesthood [meaning the new and everlasting covenant of marriage]" (D&C 131:1–2).

Many of our *family duties* flow from temple sealings and undeniably rest upon us, hence we are often "exhorted" to conscientiously "attend to all family duties" (D&C 20:47). How often we need to feel the whiplash wisdom in these words, "No other success can compensate for failure in the home"![6] How can we expect to enjoy eternally that which we neglect in mortality?

The culminating requirement repeatedly stated in the scriptures is that we must endure to the end: "And as many as . . . endure to the end, the same shall be saved" (D&C 18:22). "And . . . if thou endure it well, God shall exalt thee on high; thou shalt triumph over all thy foes" (D&C 121:8).

These ordinances and covenants (sincerely and worthily received and conscientiously revered and attended to) hasten the development of the essential qualities, already introduced, which are to be developed if we are to qualify for eternal life.

Among the perfect attributes of our living God, one that is and will be a great blessing to us, is His generosity. Important though it is, this quality is one that tends to be less noted.

God's generosity is associated with divine gladness, such as is evoked when His children keep His commandments. He is quick to bless and is delighted to honor the faithful (see D&C 76:5). God's generosity is expressed also in His long-suffering, His being always ready to respond when His children are inclined to "feel after Him" (see Acts 17:27; D&C 112:13).

The lesser but still impressive mortal examples of generosity remind and guide us as regards our need to show generosity. Consider, for instance, the exceptional generosity of the innocent Sir Thomas More, as shown in his last words to his enemies—those who had accused and convicted him—*after* they had unjustly sentenced him to be beheaded:

> Like the Blessed Apostle St. Paul, as we read in the Acts of the Apostles, was present, and consented to the death of St. Stephen, and kept their clothes that stoned him to death, and yet be they now both twain Holy Saints in heaven, and shall continue there friends for ever, so I verily trust and shall therefore right heartily pray, that though

your lordships have now here in earth been judges to my condemnation, we may yet hereafter in heaven merrily all meet together, to our everlasting salvation.[7]

President Brigham Young advised members of the Church who had been unjustly persecuted and driven to be generous in their perspectives of their particular afflictions. "If we did not exactly deserve it, there have been times when we did deserve it. If we did not deserve it at the time, it was good for [us] and gave us an experience."[8]

Generosity is needed, therefore, in how each of us manages present feelings about any past wrongs done to us. In 1866, in the Bowery on Temple Square, Brigham Young reflected on the drivings and persecutions of the Church that he had just heard recited by a previous speaker. But in Brigham, any earlier resentment had been replaced by later generosity: "I am thankful that the rehearsal of those occurrences has ceased to irritate me as it did formerly."[9] President Young had risen above the harsh memories of the history. He did not let yesterday hold tomorrow hostage. There was a willingness on his part to forget. Forgetting facilitates the generosity that springs from Christlike charity.

Brigham also wisely counseled regarding what should be our attitudes amid the adversities of life:

> These are happy days to the Saints, and we should rejoice in them; they are the best days we ever saw; and in the midst of the sorrows and afflictions of this life, its trials and temptations, the buffetings of Satan, the weakness of the flesh, and the power of death which is sown in it, there is no necessity for any mortal man to live a single day without rejoicing, and being filled with gladness. . . . We rejoice because the Lord is ours, because we are sown in weakness for the express purpose of attaining to greater power and perfection. In every thing the Saints may rejoice—in persecution, because it is necessary to purge them, and prepare the wicked for their doom; in sickness and in pain, though they are hard to bear, because we are thereby made acquainted with pain, with sorrow, and with every affliction that mortals can endure, for by contrast all things are demonstrated to our senses. . . . I rejoice that I am poor, because I shall be made rich; that I am afflicted, because I shall be comforted, and prepared to enjoy the felicity of perfect happiness, for it is impossible to properly appreciate happiness, except by enduring the opposite.[10]

Thus described and recommended is discipleship in which "afflictions . . . were swallowed up in the joy of Christ" (Alma 31:38). Part of enduring well is trusting in the Lord sufficiently that we avoid yielding to the temptation of "reviling . . . against revilers" (D&C 19:30). Not only are we to abstain from reviling, but further, as the Savior said, we are even to strive to love our enemies and to pray for them (see Matthew 5:44). Doing this is hard work, however. It requires considerable enduring to deal successfully with any insensitive or outrageous acting out by enemies! Yet the more we have "charity, the pure love of Christ," the less ego driven we will be. Likewise, the absence of excessive ego will enhance our empathy towards others, thereby facilitating our having generosity toward them.

We see loving generosity, too, in the way in which the Prophet Joseph Smith forgave the betrayer and defector William W. Phelps, when the latter desired to return. Wrote Joseph:

> Come on, dear brother, since the war is past,
> For friends at first, are friends again at last.[11]

We should welcome the returnees in our time just as William W. Phelps was welcomed back, genuinely and optimistically.

We see generosity as well in the communicative ways of two leaders in the Book of Mormon, Pahoran and Moroni, who might easily have ended up bitterly misunderstanding each other. Instead, through extra efforts to communicate, they were reconciled. Consider the stout words of Moroni in his critical epistle to Pahoran: "Behold, I am Moroni, your chief captain. I seek not for power, but to pull it down. I seek not for honor of the world, but for the glory of my God, and the freedom and welfare of my country. And thus I close mine epistle." (Alma 60:36.)

Pahoran responded empathically and generously, detailing challenges he faced of which Moroni was not aware: "Behold, I say unto you Moroni, that I do not joy in your great afflictions, yea, it grieves my soul. . . . And now, in your epistle you have censured me, but it mattereth not; I am not angry, but do rejoice in the greatness of your heart. I, Pahoran, do not seek for power, save only to retain my judgment seat that I may preserve the rights and liberty of my people. My soul standeth fast in that liberty in the which God hath made us free." (Alma 61:2, 9.)

By way of applying generosity, can we too absorb unjust criticism and persecution and say with Pahoran, "it mattereth not"?

The Moffatt translation of Paul's great epistle on charity (see 1 Corinthians chapter 13) gives us useful and relevant renderings: "Love is never glad when others go wrong." "Love makes no parade." We too should learn how to give "a soft answer [that] turneth away wrath" (Proverbs 15:1). Such a response from us may make a vital difference in another person's capacity to endure his or her situation well. Since we are only in competition with our old selves, why should we be "glad when others go wrong"?

Another virtue required of us is to be *meek*: "and becometh a saint . . . meek, humble" (Mosiah 3:19). Meekness matters greatly, and its absence shapes many situations adversely.

Conversely, note the ego dripping from only four lines—two *me*'s and four *I*'s: "And I, the Lord God, spake unto Moses, saying: That Satan, whom thou hast commanded in the name of mine Only Begotten, is the same which was from the beginning, and he came before me, saying—Behold, here am I, send me, I will be thy son, and I will redeem all mankind, that one soul shall not be lost, and surely I will do it; wherefore give me thine honor" (Moses 4:1).

Ego trips are almost always made on someone else's expense account. Noteworthy too is the fact that the proud, as in one of Jesus' parables, trust "in themselves that they [are] righteous, and [despise] others" (Luke 18:9).

The larger and the more untamed a person's ego, the greater the likelihood of that person's being offended, especially upon tasting his portion of vinegar and gall or upon encountering irony, the hard crust on the bread of adversity. Understandably, protesting words may issue: "Why me?" "Why this?" "Why now?" It is hoped, however, even if we utter such words momentarily, that we will not give way to inconsolability. From inconsolability it is a surprisingly short distance to bitterness.

Amid life's varied ironies we may begin to wonder: "Didn't God notice this torturous turn of events? And if He noticed, why did He permit it? Am I not valued? Didn't I deserve better?" Our planning usually does not allow for adverse and intruding events, which first elbow aside and then evict that which we had anticipated and perhaps even earned. Hence we can be offended by events as well as by people.

No wonder we are to be *patient* (see Mosiah 3:19). We are to be patiently submissive, even "willing to submit to all things which the Lord seeth fit to inflict upon him, even as a child doth submit to his father" (Mosiah 3:19).

We are to be *pure*: "For they shall be purified, even as I am pure" (D&C 35:21). "And all the pure in heart that shall come into it shall see God" (D&C 97:16). "For I will raise up unto myself a pure people, that will serve me in righteousness" (D&C 100:16). Chastening can result in purifying, including the purifying of our motives and intentions.

We are to be *merciful*: "Be ye therefore merciful, as your Father also is merciful" (Luke 6:36). "Blessed are the merciful: for they shall obtain mercy" (Matthew 5:7).

We are to be *forgiving*: "But if ye forgive not men their trespasses, neither will your Father forgive your trespasses" (Matthew 6:15). "I, the Lord, will forgive whom I will forgive, but of you it is required to forgive all men" (D&C 64:10).

Discipleship is thus a process of applying fundamental gospel principles while being "anxiously engaged" in *knowing*, *doing*, and *becoming*, including *receiving*, *honoring*, and *renewing* vital ordinances and covenants in a living Church through which the power of godliness is "manifest unto men in the flesh" (D&C 84:21).

"In process of time" wisely spent, we come to know God and Jesus Christ, and "this is life eternal" (John 17:3). Doing leads to knowing, and vice versa (see John 7:17; see also Alma 32:33–34). We also come to have sufficient "faith unto repentance," thereby becoming willing "to give away all [our] sins to know [God]" (Alma 34:15; 22:18). These may include activities and endeavors that distract and deflect us. Getting used to giving away such onerous things is a necessary first step to prepare us for the giving that constitutes eventual consecration.

5

PURSUING
CONSECRATION

For how knoweth a man the master whom he has not served,
and who is a stranger unto him, and is far from the thoughts
and intents of his heart? (Mosiah 5:13.)

If we were not serious about our submissiveness to God, could we endure his showing us our weaknesses? And if we did not really love Him, could we really trust Him enough to endure being tutored by Him; especially until our grinding and reminding weaknesses become emancipating strengths?

Through counsel, Church service, experience, and especially by means of the Holy Ghost, we become keenly conscious of all we yet lack (see Matthew 19:20; Mark 10:21; Ether 2:14; D&C 9:5–7).

The responsibility for pursuing discipleship, for enduring in this precious process, rests with each of us. Fortunately, this process of applying fundamental principles in our lives is self-reinforcing and self-verifying, for "every principle God has revealed carries its own convictions of its truth."[1] But how can we reliably come to know how we are doing? "How shall we know that we obey Him? There is but one method by which we can know it, and that is by the inspiration of the Spirit of the Lord witnessing unto our spirit that we are His, that we love Him, and that He loves us. It is by the spirit of revelation we know this. We have no witness to ourselves *internally*, without the spirit of revelation. We have no witness *outwardly* only by obedience to the ordinances."[2]

In the third lecture on faith we read that a person's faith will be "imperfect and unproductive" unless he believes God "actually exists," has a "correct idea" of God's character, and finally has "an actual knowledge that the course of life he is pursuing is according to [God's] will."[3]

The "spirit of revelation" to which Brigham refers is another manifestation of God's generosity. It is a vital gift. As an illustration, as far as we now know there was only one sermon for which the Prophet Joseph Smith prepared a text beforehand. It contained a significantly different rendering of two words in Paul's epistle to the Hebrews (11:6).[4] This rendering does not appear in the Joseph Smith Translation of the Bible, since the sermon was given several years after his translation of the Bible began.

In the King James Version of the Bible, Paul's words say that we cannot please God without faith and "that he is a *rewarder of* them that diligently seek him" (Hebrews 11:6). Surely God does *reward* the faithful, but Joseph Smith changed the rendering of the key word to read that the living God "is a *revealer to* them that diligently seek him." The use of the word *revealer* fits with the context, as illustrated by Paul's statement that Enoch, "before his translation . . . had this testimony, that he pleased God" (Hebrews 11:5). God *revealed* His mind to Enoch. How else could Enoch have known for certain that he pleased God?

The different rendering is of theological and salvational importance. It confirms the pattern of an omniscient and living God who is a revealer to the faithful (see Amos 3:7).

Some have sincere faith in the existence of a God but not necessarily in a revealing and omniscient God. Other sincere individuals question God's omniscience, wondering, even though respectfully, whether even God can know the future. But an omniscient and revealing God can at any present moment disclose things future. This is possible because "in the presence of God, . . . all things for their glory are manifest, past, present, and future, and are continually before the Lord" (D&C 130:7). Thus God "knoweth all things, for all things are present before [his] eyes" (D&C 38:2). He told Moses, "There is no God beside me, and all things are present with me, for I know them all" (Moses 1:6).

No qualifiers on the scope of God's knowledge appear in holy writ. Instead, we read: "O how great the holiness of our God! For he knoweth all things, and there is not anything save he knows it." (2 Nephi 9:20.)

King Benjamin, therefore, exhorts us to a humility that acknowledges not only God's existence but also His supernal capacity for comprehending: "Believe in God; believe that he is, and that he created all things, both in heaven and in earth; believe that he has all wisdom, and all power, both in heaven and in earth; believe that man doth not comprehend all the things which the Lord can comprehend" (Mosiah 4:9). Clearly, we mortals cannot fully comprehend His omniscience (see Alma 26:35).

In His mortal messiahship Jesus demonstrated this same revelatory process. He knew the thoughts of those He confronted: "But he knew their thoughts, and said to the man which had the withered hand, Rise up, and stand forth in the midst. And he arose and stood forth." (Luke 6:8.)

Jesus revealed certain things to the believing woman of Samaria concerning her life: "And many of the Samaritans of that city believed on him for the saying of the woman, which testified, He told me all that ever I did" (John 4:39). His discernment was remarkable: "But Jesus did not commit himself unto them, because he knew all men, and needed not that any should testify of man: for he knew what was in man" (John 2:24–25).

No wonder Jesus "needed not that any man should teach him" (JST, Matthew 3:25).

Our loving, living, and revealing Father God is thus very different from an unknown and unknowing deity who is substantially disconnected from and uncommunicative with His children on the earth (see Acts 17:21–30). A revealing, tutoring God, however, will reveal His secrets to His prophets, but likewise to all who please Him, according to their stations and individual needs (see Amos 3:7; D&C 1:20).

God rescues, and even intervenes at times, in order to aid the faithful, as set forth in Paul's litany of examples in chapter 11 of Hebrews. Indeed, God does *reward* the faithful, but sometimes that reward is expressed in what He chooses to reveal to them. Thus the closer we are to the living God and the more helpful in building the living Church, the more He will reveal to us, and the greater His help to us as we strive to endure it well. Of course, revelations for the entire Church come only through the prophets, ordained and sustained, who stand at the head of the Church.

Jesus' invitation to come to "know" Him by doing contains this promise: "Take my yoke upon you, and learn of me; for I am

meek and lowly in heart: and ye shall find rest unto your souls"
(Matthew 11:29).

This process brings not only confirmation as a result of our
faithfulness but also revelation to guide us in our personal lives and
callings. God sees the end from the beginning and can communicate to us who are in the muddled, mortal middle. Hence we need
faith in Him in order to learn from Him. As our faith pleases Him,
He can *reward us and reveal to us,* for He delights to honor those
who serve Him—especially those who are seriously pursuing consecration (see D&C 6:5).

Achieving greater consecration by receiving the necessary
ordinances, making and keeping the necessary covenants, understanding the necessary doctrines, and ever becoming more and
more the man or the woman of Christ is a tall order in any age,
but particularly in today's secular world. Once again, therefore, it
is imperative for us to know that we truly are the spirit sons and
daughters of the living God, loved and overseen by Him in the
midst of the vastness of His creations. Identity precedes felicity. He
cares for each one of us and has assured us of this resplendent reality many times and in many ways.

If we understand the vibrant plan of salvation of the living
God, we will understand too why it is that He loves us enough to
remodel and to stretch us. C. S. Lewis's metaphor, paraphrasing
George Macdonald's, remains one of the very best:

> Imagine yourself as a living house. God comes in to rebuild that
> house. At first, perhaps, you can understand what He is doing. He is
> getting the drains right and stopping the leaks in the roof and so on:
> you knew that those jobs needed doing and so you are not surprised.
> But presently he starts knocking the house about in a way that hurts
> abominably and does not seem to make sense. What on earth is He
> up to? The explanation is that He is building quite a different house
> from the one you thought of—throwing out a new wing here,
> putting on an extra floor there, running up towers, making court-
> yards. You thought you were going to be made into a decent little
> cottage: but He is building a palace.[5]

Among some Church members there is, sad to say, a lack of
real faith in the living God and in His plan of salvation. This
includes the universal need for repentance and remodeling; failure
to pay a full tithing; failure to wear the holy temple garments;

refusal to work meekly at making a marriage more successful or helping a family to become happier; inordinate resentment of personal trials; trying to serve the Lord without offending the devil or the world; being willing to serve the Lord but only in an advisory capacity; failing to sustain the Brethren; neglecting prayer; neglecting holy scriptures; neglecting parents; neglecting neighbors; neglecting sacrament meetings; neglecting temple attendance; and so on. Of such happiness-draining failures the common cause, at the testing point, is the failure to endure it well. When we stop short, we interrupt the precious process of personal development.

If we endure it well, however, and do not "faint in our minds," our performance is finally sanctifying, being "consecrated for the welfare of [our] soul" (Hebrews 12:3; 2 Nephi 32:9).

Whenever Church members speak of consecration it should be done reverently, while acknowledging that each of us comes "short of the glory of God," some of us far short (Romans 3:23). Even the conscientious have not arrived, but they sense the shortfall and are genuinely striving. It is consoling that God's grace flows not only to those "who love [Him] and keep all [His] commandments," but likewise to those "that [seek] so to do" (D&C 46:9).

A second group of members are "honorable" but not "valiant" (see D&C 76:75, 79). They are not really aware of the gap or of the importance of closing it. These "honorable" individuals are certainly not miserable or wicked, nor are they unrighteous and unhappy. It is not what they have done but what they have left undone that is amiss. For example, if valiant, they could touch others deeply instead of merely being remembered pleasantly.

In a third group are those who are grossly entangled with the "ungodliness" of the world, reminding us all, as Peter wrote, that if "[we are] overcome" by something worldly, "[we are] brought in bondage" (2 Peter 2:19).

If one "mind[s] the things of the flesh" (Romans 8:5), he cannot "have the mind of Christ" (1 Corinthians 2:16), because his thought patterns are "far from" Jesus, as are the desires or the "intents of his heart" (Mosiah 5:13). It is ironic that, if the Master is a stranger to us, we will merely end up serving other masters. The sovereignty of these other masters is real even if it sometimes is subtle, for they do call their cadence. Actually, "we are all enlisted,"[6] if only in the ranks of the indifferent.

To the extent that we are not willing to be led by the Lord we will be driven by our appetites, or we will be greatly preoccupied with the lesser things of the day. The remedy is implicit in the marvelous lamentation of King Benjamin: "For how knoweth a man the master whom he has not served, and who is a stranger unto him, and is far from the thoughts and intents of his heart?" (Mosiah 5:13.) For many moderns, sad to say, the query "What think ye of Christ?" (Matthew 22:42) would be answered, "I really don't think of Him at all"!

Consider three examples of how otherwise honorable people in the Church keep back a portion and thus prevent greater consecration (see Acts 5:1–4).

A sister gives commendable, visible civic service. Yet even with her good image in the community, she remains a comparative stranger to Jesus' holy temples and His holy scriptures, two vital dimensions of discipleship. But she could have Christ's image in her countenance (see Alma 5:14).

An honorable father, dutifully involved in the cares of his family, is less than kind and gentle with individual family members. He is a comparative stranger to Jesus' gentleness and kindness, which we are instructed to emulate, whereas a little more effort by this father would make a large difference.

Consider the returned missionary, skills polished while serving an honorable mission, striving earnestly for success in his career. Busy, he ends up in a posture of some accommodation with the world. Thus he forgoes building up the kingdom first and instead builds up himself. A small course correction now would make a large, even destinational, difference for him later on.

These deficiencies just illustrated are those of omission. Once the telestial sins are left behind and thenceforth avoided, the focus falls ever more upon the sins of omission. These omissions signify a lack of qualifying fully for the celestial kingdom (see Exodus 20:8, 12). Only greater consecration can correct these omissions, which have consequences just as real as do the sins of commission. Many of us thus have sufficient faith to avoid the major sins of commission but not enough faith to sacrifice our distracting obsessions or to focus on our omissions.

Most omissions occur because we fail to get outside ourselves. We are so busy checking on our own temperatures that we do not notice the burning fevers of others even when we could offer them some of the needed remedies, such as encouragement, kindness, and commendation. The hands that hang down and most need to be lifted up belong to those too discouraged even to reach out anymore.

Actually, everything depends—initially and finally—on our desires. These shape our thought patterns. Our desires thus precede our deeds and lie at the very cores of our souls, tilting us toward or away from God (see D&C 4:3). God can "educate our desires."[7] Others seek to manipulate our desires. But it is we who form the desires, the "thoughts and intents of [our] hearts" (Mosiah 5:13).

The end rule is "according to [our] desires . . . shall it be done unto [us]" (D&C 11:17), "for I, the Lord, will judge all men according to their works, according to the desire of their hearts" (D&C 137:9; see also Alma 41:5; D&C 6:20, 27). A person's individual will thus remains uniquely his. God will not override it or overwhelm it. Hence we'd better want the consequences of what we want!

Another cosmic fact: only by aligning our wills with God's is full happiness to be found. Anything less results in a lesser portion (see Alma 12:10–11). The Lord will work with us even if, at first, we "can no more than desire" but are willing to "give place for a portion of [His] words" (Alma 32:27). A small foothold is all He needs. But we must desire and provide it.

Many of us are kept from eventual consecration because we mistakenly think that, somehow, by letting our will be swallowed up in the will of God we lose our individuality (see Mosiah 15:7). What we are really worried about, of course, is giving up not self but selfish things—like our roles, our time, our preeminence, and our possessions. No wonder we are instructed by the Savior to lose ourselves (see Luke 9:24). He is only asking us to lose the old self in order to find the new self. It is a question not of one's losing identity but of finding one's true identity. It is ironic that many people already lose themselves anyway in their consuming hobbies and preoccupations that are far, far lesser things.

Ever observant in both the first and second estates, consecrated Jesus always knew in which direction He faced: He consistently emulated His Father: "The Son can do nothing of himself, but what he seeth the Father do: for what things soever he doeth, these also doeth the Son likewise" (John 5:19); for "I have

suffered the will of the Father in all things from the beginning"
(3 Nephi 11:11).

As one's will is increasingly submissive to the will of God, he
can receive inspiration and revelation so much needed to help
meet the trials of life. For Abraham, first came the "impossible"
promise—though he was a hundred years old and Sarah ninety,
well past the child-bearing age, a son would be born to them. Paul
notes that at this, faithful Abraham "staggered not . . . through
unbelief" (Romans 4:20). Years later God commanded Abraham
to offer that son, Isaac, as a sacrifice. Of that trying and defining
episode, John Taylor observed that "nothing but the spirit of revelation could have given him this confidence, and . . . sustained
him under these peculiar circumstances."[8]

Will we, too, trust the Lord amid a perplexing trial for which
we have no easy explanation? Do we understand—really comprehend—that Jesus knows and understands when we are stressed and
perplexed? The complete consecration which effected the Atonement ensured Jesus' perfect empathy; He felt our very pains and
afflictions before we did and knows how to succor us (see Alma
7:11–12; 2 Nephi 9:21). Since the most innocent one suffered the
most, our own cries of "Why?" cannot match His. But we can
utter the same, submissive word: "Nevertheless . . ." (Matthew
26:39).

Progression toward submission confers another blessing: an
enhanced capacity for joy. Counseled President Brigham Young,
"If you want to enjoy exquisitely, become a Latter-day Saint, and
then live the doctrine of Jesus Christ."[9]

Thus consecration is not resignation or a mindless caving in.
Rather, it is a deliberate expanding outward, making us more honest when we sing, "More used would I be."[10] Consecration, likewise, is not shoulder-shrugging acceptance but, instead, shoulder-
squaring to better bear the yoke.

Consecration involves pressing forward "with a steadfastness
in Christ" with a "brightness of hope, and a love of God and of all
men . . . [while] feasting on the word of Christ" (2 Nephi 31:20).
Jesus pressed forward sublimely. He did not shrink, such as by
going only 60 percent of the distance toward the full atonement.
Instead, He "finished [His] preparations" for all mankind, bringing a universal resurrection—not one in which 40 percent of us
would have been left out (see D&C 19:18–19).

Each of us might well ask, "In what ways am I shrinking or holding back?" Meek introspection may yield some bold insights. For example, we can tell much by what we have already willingly discarded along the pathway of discipleship. It is the only pathway where littering is permissible, even encouraged. In the early stages the debris left behind includes the grosser sins of commission. Later debris differs; the things being discarded are those that have caused the misuse or under use of our time and talent.

Along this pathway leading to consecration, stern and unsought challenges sometimes hasten us in a jettisoning that is needed if we are to achieve increased consecration (see Helaman 12:3). If we have grown soft, hard times may be necessary. If we are too contented, a dose of divine discontent may come. A relevant insight may be contained in reproof. A new calling beckons us away from comfortable routines wherein the needed competencies have already been developed. One may be stripped of accustomed luxury so that the malignant mole of materialism may be removed. One may be scorched by humiliation so that pride can be melted away. Whatever we lack will get attention, one way or another.

John Taylor indicated that the Lord may even choose to wrench our very heartstrings.[11] If our hearts are set too much upon the things of this world, they may need to be wrenched, or broken, or undergo a mighty change (see Alma 5:12).

Consecration is thus both a principle and a process and is not tied to a single moment. Instead, it is freely given, drop by drop, until the cup of consecration brims and finally runs over.

Long before that, however, as Jesus declared, we must "settle this in [our] hearts" that we will do what He asks of us (JST, Luke 14:28). President Young further counseled us "to submit to the hand of the Lord, . . . and acknowledge his hand in all things, . . . then you will be exactly right; and until you come to that point, you cannot be entirely right. That is what we have to come to."[12]

Thus acknowledging God's hand includes, in the words of the Prophet Joseph, trusting that God has made "ample provision" beforehand to achieve all His purposes, including His purposes in our lives.[13] Sometimes He clearly directs; at other times it seems He merely permits some things to happen. Therefore we will not always understand the role of God's hand, but we know enough of His heart and mind to be submissive. Thus when we are perplexed and stressed, explanatory help is not always immediately forthcoming, but compensatory help will be. Our process of cognition gives way to our personal submission, as we experience those moments when we learn to internalize the words of the psalm, "Be still, and know that I am God" (Psalm 46:10).

Then, the more one's will is thus "swallowed up," the more one's afflictions, rather than necessarily being removed, will be "swallowed up in the joy of Christ" (Alma 31:38).

Seventy years ago, Lord Moulton coined a perceptive phrase, "obedience to the unenforceable," describing "the obedience of a man to that which he cannot be forced to obey."[14] God's blessings, including those associated with consecration, come by unforced obedience to the laws upon which they are predicated (see D&C 130:20–21). Thus our deepest desires determine our degree of "obedience to the unenforceable." God seeks to have us become more consecrated, by giving everything. Then, when we come home to Him, He will generously give us "all that [He] hath" (see D&C 84:38).

The submission of one's will is placing on God's altar the only uniquely personal thing one has to place there. The many other things we "give" are actually the things He has already given or loaned to us. However, when we finally submit ourselves by letting our individual wills be swallowed up in God's will, we will really be giving something to Him! It is the only possession which is truly ours to give. Consecration thus constitutes the only unconditional surrender which is also a total victory.

We need all the help we can get along the road to ultimate consecration. It is a happy thought that the living God has provided us with a "great cloud of witnesses," some contemporary examples and many from the scriptures and history, to encourage and assist us.

6

LIVING AMID SO GREAT A CLOUD OF WITNESSES

Search the scriptures; for . . . they are they which testify of me (John 5:39).

And I did read many things unto them which were written in the books of Moses; . . . for I did liken all scriptures unto us, that it might be for our profit and learning (1 Nephi 19:23).

Jesus directs us to "search the scriptures" primarily because they testify of Him and of what He did, as our Savior, in the great atonement. They also testify of His matchless character[1] (see John 5:39). Without Christ's character and His remarkable capacity to endure it well, His performance of the astonishing atonement with its resulting blessing of a universal resurrection would not have been possible. No wonder the Book of Mormon instructs us that we are to preach of Christ, talk of Christ, and rejoice in Christ, so that our children may know to whom they may look (2 Nephi 25:26).

It is important that the scriptures and likewise Church history also provide window-like verses and inspiring and instructive episodes that permit us to access and be affected by a "cloud of witnesses" (Hebrews 12:1). Thereby we can look into the souls of these great men and women who testified of Jesus and whom He tutored. These growth models testify to us, too, by the eloquence of their examples, which we can "liken" unto ourselves.

They endured their own difficult moments, as we are called on to do. They too experienced conceptual inadequacy and endured feelings of personal inadequacy. But they still trusted in the Lord. They too needed respite, renewals through time and space, in order to endure: "And he said unto them, Come ye yourselves apart into a desert place, and rest a while: for there were many coming and going, and they had no leisure so much as to eat. And they departed into a desert place by ship privately." (Mark 6:31–32.) Likening holy scriptures and historical episodes unto ourselves is, therefore, essential if they are to be fully for "our profit and learning."

Such glimpses into the souls of great men and women abundantly confirm how rigorous discipleship is, even for the advanced students. It becomes repeatedly apparent, too, how crucial it is for us to trust the Lord when we do not fully understand, when we feel inadequate, or when we are deprived in some particular respect and cannot help but notice and compare. The cloud of witnesses will keep present earthly things in perspective.

While being remodeled and stretched, will we, for example, learn from Enoch's excellent example how better to trust the Lord? Enoch was "but a lad," the "people hated" him, and he was "slow of speech." Someday we shall know and appreciate more what Enoch endured in those and in other respects (see Moses 6:31). Jesus tutored and trained submissive Enoch, who then established the matchless city of Enoch and led its people on to unique spiritual glory (see Moses 7:18, 21–23).

Enoch actually saw the "God of heaven . . . weep" over needless human misery (Moses 7:28–37). When Enoch was shown a portion of human wickedness, he reacted with anguish. This resulted in a major lesson in theodicy for all of us concerning the interplay of human agency and misery and why God permits it. (See Moses 7:32–37.)

Enoch at first "had bitterness of soul," refusing to be comforted. Then the Lord showed him Jesus' great rescuing and redeeming atonement, which was to be accomplished in the meridian of time. (See Moses 7:44, 46–47.)

We mortals should never think, even for a moment, that (despite all the cumulative pictures of human suffering around the globe we see on TV) we have glimpsed more than the smallest, surface part of human suffering that God sees in its entirety. Furthermore, God knows perfectly the depth as well as the massive quantity of that suffering. Our reactions to human suffering cannot even approach His. No wonder, given our lesser bearing capacities, that God in His wisdom and mercy will shorten the days before his rescuing Son comes again to put an end to human tragedies (see Matthew 24:22).

Yet even with our own lesser witnessing of human wickedness and suffering, faith in Christ's atonement and the Father's plan still provides the only final and full comfort. This will be especially the case amid the difficult events that will precede the Savior's second coming.

Part of the comfort of those days as of these is the reassurance that God's purposes will prevail. The Prophet Joseph assured us that God lives in an "eternal now," because "the past, the present, and the future" are before Him continually.[2] Unlike us, He sees the end from the beginning. In His plan, God has anticipated human errors and wickedness and has made "adequate provision" for them. Thus all of God's purposes will finally be achieved. How vital, therefore, for us to have enduring faith in the Father's plan of salvation!

That kind of faith has to compensate for the incompleteness of our understanding. Because of that inadequacy we do not always know immediately and precisely what we should pray for. In his prayers, Paul experienced what some of us occasionally experience, as in this instructive disclosure: "For we know not what we should pray for as we ought: but the Spirit itself maketh intercession for us with groanings which cannot be uttered" (Romans 8:26).

On his arrival in Macedonia, Paul was physically weary and had to endure being "troubled on every side; without were fightings, within were fears"; understandably he felt "cast down." (2 Corinthians 7:5–6.) Nevertheless he described the divine consolation and comfort he received. From intensive and varied experiences, Paul knew what it was like to be troubled, distressed, and perplexed. Yet he wrote reassuringly that nothing can separate us from the love of Christ, not tribulation, distress, persecution, famine, perils, or the sword (see Romans 8:35). He knew to whom to look for consolation and perspective.

In his soliloquy, Nephi, though righteous and diligent, felt his inadequacies; his soul drooped in the valley of sorrow (see 2 Nephi 4:26, 28). He gratefully recited his many blessings, yet still felt that he fell short. We too, while feeling much blessed, nevertheless may feel very inadequate. Our solution is Nephi's solution; we should resolve to continue to rejoice, declaring: "I have trusted in thee, and I will trust in thee forever" (2 Nephi 4:34).

At times Nephi, like Paul, was perplexed. Nevertheless he modeled for us when he trustingly said, "I know that [God] loveth his children; nevertheless, I do not know the meaning of all things" (1 Nephi 11:17). For us in this time of "distress of nations, with perplexity," gospel perspective is vital if we are to endure it well.

We will not always know the full meaning of what is happening to us or around us, but like Nephi we can still know that God loves us personally and will see us through our difficult or down times (see 1 Nephi 11:23).

Mary, in the midst of her wonderment at the birth of Jesus, needed time to ponder all that the visiting shepherds and others had said. So she trusted; and "Mary kept all these things and pondered them in her heart" (Luke 2:19). Bright and perceptive, Mary still doubtless found, as did Alma, that she could not "speak the smallest part" of what she felt (Alma 26:16).

With the Restoration, more scriptural windows and clouds of witnesses are provided. In addition to the Holy Bible we have the Book of Mormon, the Doctrine and Covenants, the Pearl of Great Price, and the Joseph Smith Translation. Restoration scriptures provide hundreds of additional pages that testify of Christ. And there will be yet another volume: "And it shall come to pass that the Jews shall have the words of the Nephites, and the Nephites shall have the words of the Jews; and the Nephites and the Jews shall have the words of the lost tribes of Israel; and the lost tribes of Israel shall have the words of the Nephites and the Jews" (2 Nephi 29:13).

And even more is to come: "We believe all that God has revealed, all that he does now reveal, and we believe that He will yet reveal many great and important things pertaining to the Kingdom of God" (Articles of Faith, 1:9).

Multiple scriptures speak of God's seeking to "convince" mortals that Jesus is the Christ: "And as I spake concerning the convincing of the Jews, that Jesus is the very Christ, it must needs be that the Gentiles be convinced also that Jesus is the Christ, the Eternal God" (2 Nephi 26:12; see also D&C 11:21; 90:10; 2 Nephi 25:18; Alma 12:7; 30:43; 3 Nephi 28:29; title page to the Book of Mormon).

The quantity of Restoration scriptures[3] is matched by their quality, their relevancy, and their purity. Jesus declared that the scriptures testify of Him; hence the greater the quantity and quality of scriptures, the greater the testimony of Jesus and likewise of the resurrection (see John 5:39). All this combines significantly and expands our "hope and views of Christ and the resurrection" (Alma 27:28).

Not only are there many such scriptural windows, but likewise witnessing windows from history are helpful in seeing an enlarged "cloud of witnesses." For instance, Brigham Young—a true and exceptional disciple but still in process—had enough faith to continue to the end his struggle to improve, including his battle with one of life's sternest challenges: "One of the hardest lessons for me to learn on earth is to love a man who hates me. . . . I do not think I have got this lesson by heart, and I do not know how long I shall have to live to learn it. I am trying."[4] We, too, must keep "trying."

Such examples can be a needed spiritual spur to us.

From time to time life will bring us difficulties, but even severe circumstances in the present need not rob us of our long-term hope and perspective. A young Eliza Snow, evicted from Nauvoo by events and now in a westbound ox wagon in the midst of cold and tribulation, still had perspective about "things as they really are" (Jacob 4:13). Eliza was "thankful that we are so well off."[5]

In the early stages of his faith, King Lamoni's father did not understand all that Aaron taught him. But he surrendered anyway, saying trustingly, "And if now thou sayest there is a God, behold I will believe" (Alma 22:7). In his first, tentative prayer, he was trusting, finally pledging to "give away all my sins to know [God]" (Alma 22:18).

Is our trust sufficient that we will surrender? Will we have faith enough to give away *all* our sins? There is only one to take them!

The Prophet Joseph was often concerned with loyal Brigham Young's poverty, which was intensified at times as a result of Brigham's devotion. Brigham once observed: "I took a mission to Canada at my own expense; and from the time that I was baptized until the day of our sorrow and affliction, at the martyrdom of Joseph and Hyrum, no summer passed over my head but what I was traveling and preaching, and the only thing I ever received from the Church, during over twelve years, and the only means that were ever given me by the Prophet, that I now recollect, was in 1842, when brother Joseph sent me the half of a small pig that the brethren had brought to him, I did not ask him for it; it weighed 93 pounds."[6] And again: "Joseph would often ask me how I lived. I told him I did not know—that I did my best, and the Lord did the rest."[7] Such exemplification amid deprivation should strengthen us.

When, for the moment, we cannot see any rescuing remedies, either, will we too do our best and let the Lord do the rest?

Just after a special neighbor, Elder Marion G. Romney, was called to serve as a Counselor in the First Presidency, he spoke in our ward fast and testimony meeting. Meek President Romney said, in substance, "I have always sustained the President of the Church, and I can sustain this President now, even when he calls me as his Counselor." It was said with great tenderness.

Will each of us likewise trust each President of the Church not only in the callings he extends but also, which is just as important, in how he calls the cadence for the Church?

While Jesus is clearly the only perfect model, His best followers also give us needed and helpful glimpses of them during their journeys, including their recoveries from their falterings. Since faltering does occur, reaching out to those who have faltered is vital to them and renewing to ourselves. Oliver Cowdery provides an example of such a precious returnee. When Elder George Smith was in Council Bluffs, Iowa, in October of 1848, he visited with a then out-of-the-Church Oliver Cowdery. In spite of his past disaffections, Oliver testified "that Joseph Smith had fulfilled his mission faithfully before until death."[8]

Oliver Cowdery was rebaptized in Kanesville, Iowa, at 2:00 p.m., on 5 November 1848. Understandably concerned with his reputation, he said: "I have sustained an honorable character before the world during my absence from you . . . a small matter with you [but] it is of vast importance. . . . I am out of the Church. I know the door into the Church, and I wish to become a member through the door. I wish to be a humble, private member. I did not come here to seek honor."[9] Oliver thus demonstrated his humble character. He was baptized by Orson Hyde, upon whom he had first conferred the priesthood years before.

Later in a letter dated January 13, 1849, to Samuel W. Richards, Oliver Cowdery continued to testify. In this instance the testimony included the restoration of the Aaronic and Melchizedek

Priesthoods, saying, "Blessed is the elder who has received the same, and thrice blessed and holy is he who shall continue to the end." In that same letter, Oliver refers to Joseph as a Seer.

In Richmond, Missouri, in 1887 David Whitmer affirmed Oliver's tenacity concerning the Book of Mormon, evidenced even on his deathbed:

> I will say once more to all mankind, that I have never at any time denied that testimony or any part thereof. I also testify to the world, that neither Oliver Cowdery or Martin Harris ever at anytime denied their testimony. . . . I was present at the death bed of Oliver Cowdery, and his last words were, "Brother David, be true to your testimony to the Book of Mormon."[10]

David Whitmer apparently was present with some of Oliver Cowdery's family members. A family member reports of Oliver that "just before he breathed his last, he asked to be raised up . . . so he could talk to the family and friends and he told them to live according to the teachings in the Book of Mormon and they would meet him in Heaven. Then he said lay me down and let me fall asleep in the arms of Jesus and he fell asleep without a struggle."[11]

When Jacob Gates visited Oliver Cowdery in 1849 on his way to England, Oliver reaffirmed his testimony of the Book of Mormon by taking down a first edition copy of that book and turning to the testimony of the Three Witnesses, which he read in a solemn manner. Jacob Gates quotes him then as saying: "Jacob, I want you to remember what I say to you. I am a dying man, and what would it profit me to tell you a lie? I know," said he, "that this Book of Mormon was translated by the gift and power of God. My eyes saw, my hears heard, and my understanding was touched, and I know that whereof I testified is true. It was no dream, no vain imagination of the mind—it was real."[12]

These and many other windows into Church history provide a way through which we can see and hear from a cloud of witnesses.

In this latter part of this last dispensation, Church leaders and missionaries travel about the globe, generally in comparative ease. Yet we would do well to remember the travails of our predecessors. Our season of service has its own stiff challenges, to be sure, but not all those faced by our predecessors.

Think, for instance, of the 1866 voyage of young B. H. Roberts across the Atlantic, when "violent storms . . . last[ed] as long as three days" compared to our brief minutes of turbulence in our otherwise comfortable jetliners.

As a boy, B.H. Roberts crossed much of the plains barefoot. "His feet became black, hard, and cracked from the journey; blood often oozed from the cracks. Sometimes at night [his sister] Mary cried in sympathy as she pulled spines of prickly pear cactus from his feet." By the time Brother Roberts arrived in Salt Lake City in September, "he was wearing a pair of boots, many sizes too large, that he had discovered in a burned out Pony Express station."[13]

Today we have language training for missionaries, and able interpreters waiting to assist us at various locations. As a young missionary, George Q. Cannon—already very homesick in Hawaii amid strange food and temporarily separated from his missionary companions—endured feeling very unconnected. Even so, President Cannon with perspective humbly and generously acknowledged of exemplars in the Book of Mormon, "What were my petty difficulties compared with those afflictions which they had to endure?"[14] We of today could well say the same of our predecessors in this dispensation.

Today's emissaries occasionally have problems with temporarily lost luggage, but on his mission to Hawaii young Elder Joseph F. Smith, because of a fire on Palawai, saw his trunk "reduced to ashes except his missionary certificate," including the "journals which he had faithfully kept." The loss to be endured included especially precious "copies of the first edition (European) of the Book of Mormon, [and] the Doctrine and Covenants, which had been given as a present to [his father] Hyrum Smith."

There was no Church travel office to pave the way for missionaries then. Instead, the missionaries often had to get employment to "earn their passage back to the United States," as did young Joseph F. Smith. He described how he travelled in lowly steerage and in the holds where "I never before smelt a smell like that smell smelt."[15]

Alma taught his son that the scriptural record the Nephites kept had "enlarged the memory of this people" (Alma 37:8). For our part, we today can "enlarge" our memories by incorporating the lessons of scriptural and Church history as if they were our own. And the Holy Ghost can be a great and needed helper as to how we can best manage our personal memories, especially when we need to be brought in remembrance of them.

History and memory can converge to settle us spiritually and deepen our determination to keep the commandments. The instructions of Jesus to His disciples, therefore, are to "settle this in your hearts, that ye will do the things which I shall teach, and command you" (JST, Luke 14:28). When we are so settled and established, we will endure whatever comes rather than be "tossed to and fro" either by false doctrines or by the fashions of the world (see Ephesians 4:14; 1 Corinthians 7:31). The cloud of witnesses can steady us and give us perspective amid today's pressing secular crowd.

Spiritual remembrance of our own relevant experiences is vital. Memory provides us with a precious capacity. It is not easy to describe what actually occurs as nostalgia stirs us productively. Abraham Lincoln spoke perceptively of "the mystic chords of memory." Thus we cannot fully account for what happens when our memories focus so intensely and positively on a particular time or event that had seemingly since slipped away from us. Suddenly we feel included again! Yet the moment is brief, for, alas, we are soon expelled—again; but only after such glimpses of the past have revived in us a fresh and vivid sense of what was, because the refreshing surf of recall rolled briefly over us. What often emerges is a growing and glowing gratitude to God.

Of human memory, scholars have written:

> The function of memory in your life is not only quite remarkable, it is vitally necessary to your survival as a human being. It is your memory that stores up your past experiences enabling you to function swiftly and automatically without "taking thought" or starting from the beginning in everything you do . . . if it were not for memory, everything you take for granted—such as remembering your own name as well as the names of your friends and relatives, the street where you live, your telephone number, where you work, driving your car, what you had for dinner—all would require the necessity of being "re-learned" or keeping endless written and taped records for constant referral.
>
> There are literally thousands of important "little" items of information and concepts in the daily routine of the average person which require remembering and automatic responses. Even the performance of the simplest activities you do—walking, talking, eating, reading, shopping, and so on and ad infinitum—are all part of your earlier conditioning and as part of your memory storehouse of "how to" information, permits you to perform countless tasks automatically and naturally without actual concentration or conscious thought.[16]

Mark Van Doren has observed: "Memory performs the impossible for man; holds together past and present, gives continuity and dignity to human life. This is the companion, this is the tutor, the poet, the library, with which you travel."[17]

We usually find it difficult, however, to share fully with others glimpses of our own past. Our enthusiasm exceeds their appreciation. Though they see how such useful nostalgia pleases us, and they are glad, it is only vicariously. Our memories are peculiarly our own. No wonder, therefore, that we sometimes resist any rejection of our particular remembrances because, in a way, rejection of our memories is a denial of our participation. We do not wish to be severed from our pasts.

Yet, as we have all experienced, an unchecked memory can unduly enhance what was reality, proceeding to "warehouse" a mere "whisper . . . as a shout."[18] We need the help of the Holy Ghost to manage our memories, preserving the relevancy and integrity of the process. Even so, how grateful we ought to be for the measured ways in which reliable examples come alive for us not only in holy scriptures but also from our own pasts!

Meanwhile, though memories can bless us, we need to go on living and enduring in the "holy present"; for, as C. S. Lewis observed, "These things—the beauty, the memory of our own past—are good images of what we really desire; but if they are mistaken for the thing itself they turn into dumb idols, breaking the hearts of their worshippers. For they are not the thing itself; they are only the scent of a flower we have not found, the echo of a tune we have not heard, news from a country we have never yet visited."[19]

A similar caution is called for as to what we choose each day to put in our storehouses of memory. It is a blessed condition if we can be nourished later therefrom rather than some day remember with regret. The words from President Joseph F. Smith are particularly relevant here: "In reality a man cannot forget anything. He may have a lapse of memory; he may not be able to recall at the moment a thing that he knows, or words that he has spoken; he may not have the power at his will to call up these events and words; but let God Almighty touch the mainspring of the memory, and awaken recollection, and you will find then that you have not even forgotten a single idle word that you have spoken."[20]

These prophetic words from a prophet of our dispensation

serve to remind us that living prophets who lead the living Church and who teach from living scriptures likewise are essential. This special combination is of great value as we strive to keep things in true remembrance and in inspired perspective.

7

FOLLOWING THE
PROPHETS

What I the Lord have spoken, I have spoken, and I excuse not myself; and though the heavens and the earth pass away, my word shall not pass away, but shall all be fulfilled, whether by mine own voice or by the voice of my servants, it is the same (D&C 1:38).

An acquaintance said to me one day: "I admire your church very much. I think I could accept everything about it—except Joseph Smith." To which I responded: "That statement is a contradiction. If you accept the revelation, you must accept the revelator." (Gordon B. Hinckley.)[1]

Accepting and following the counsel of the Lord's prophets helps us greatly to endure well. This includes following the wise and inspired prophets in this dispensation. These men also exemplify for us in various ways, including by their quality of endurance. Who can forget the many exemplary ways in which Presidents Spencer W. Kimball, Ezra Taft Benson, and Howard W. Hunter, each beset with physical afflictions and over extended periods of time, nevertheless managed to endure it well? How can we measure the contagiousness of such examples?

Among so many instructive utterances, here are but a few illustrations of prophetic teachings bearing on endurance. These are taken only from the second and fifteenth Presidents of the Church, President Brigham Young and President Gordon B. Hinckley, respectively.

President Hinckley, who has known personally eight—a majority—of the latter-day prophets thus far, testifies of how, among other things, each endured "a long period of experience and tempering, of training and discipline to stand as an instrument of the Almighty in speaking to the people for their blessing and direction."

Of the Prophet Joseph, President Hinckley has said: "I have not spoken face to face with all of the prophets of this dispensation. I was not acquainted with the Prophet Joseph Smith, nor did I ever hear him speak. My grandfather, who as a young man lived in Nauvoo, did hear him and testified of his divine calling as the great prophet of this dispensation. But I feel I have come to know the Prophet Joseph Smith."[2]

Ira Nathaniel Hinckley, President Hinckley's valiant grandfather just referred to, became a relatively young pioneer and endured much, being no stranger to adversity. In the April 1995 general conference, President Hinckley, understandably moved while so doing, recited this account of ancestral endurance:

> My grandfather as a boy was baptized in the summer of 1836 in Ontario, Canada. His widowed mother eventually brought her two boys to Springfield, Illinois. From there, my grandfather walked to Nauvoo, where he listened to the Prophet Joseph Smith. When the exodus of our people occurred in 1846, he was an eighteen-year-old youth of strength and capacity and faith. He was a skilled builder of wagons and a blacksmith. He was among those whom President Young requested to remain for a time in Iowa to assist those still on the westward trail. He married in 1848 and set out for this valley in the spring of 1850.
>
> Somewhere along that wearisome trail, his young wife sickened and died. With his own hands he dug a grave, split logs to make a coffin, lovingly buried her, then tearfully took their eleven-month-old child in his arms and marched on to this valley.[3]

A few years later Ira was back, posted on the pioneer trail, helping immigrants. Though sick in bed for several preceding days, Ira rose to help others. He wrote in his journal: "I had forgot that I was sick. For there was no time for being sick."[4] A short while later, back in Salt Lake City, Ira heard Brigham Young speak "on the principle of resigning our will to the will of our Father in heaven [that we might] become one." Ira, meek and submissive, must have understood the sermon well!

Many people think primarily of Brigham Young as a great colonizer and a governor, and excellent he was in those roles. But

Brigham, much more than a colonizer and a governor, was a seer and a profound teacher of gospel doctrines and principles. He had developed to a high degree his own capacity to endure it well, out of which experiences he could authentically encourage other Church members to do likewise.

Brigham noted, for instance, that he had to endure certain inconveniences in order to harvest from the Prophet Joseph much of what Brigham taught in the decades to follow: "In my experience I never did let an opportunity pass of getting with the Prophet Joseph and of hearing him speak in public or in private, so that I might draw understanding from the fountain from which he spoke, that I might have it and bring it forth when it was needed. . . . In the days of the Prophet Joseph, such moments were more precious to me than all the wealth of the world. No matter how great my poverty—if I had to borrow meal to feed my wife and children, I never let an opportunity pass of learning what the Prophet had to impart."[5]

Brigham Young also successfully endured a temptation to which others succumbed: to criticize the Prophet Joseph. He said: "I never called him in question, even in my feelings, for an act of his, except once. I did not like his policy in a matter, and a feeling came into my heart that would have led me to complain; but it was much shorter lived than Jonah's gourd, for it did not last half a minute. Much of Joseph's policy in temporal things was different from my ideas of the way to manage them. He did the best he could, and I do the best I can."[6]

Only once, and then on a trivial and passing matter, President Young experienced a momentary "want of confidence in Brother Joseph Smith. . . . It was not concerning religious matters . . . it was in relation to his financiering—to his managing the temporal affairs which he undertook. . . . [I] understood, by the spirit of revelation manifested to me, that if I was to harbour a thought in my heart that Joseph could be wrong in anything, I would begin to lose confidence in him, and that feeling would grow from step to step, and from one degree to another."[7]

Reflecting what must have been his deep and frequent pondering of large matters, Brigham Young had a special sense of how deep God's commitment is to our moral agency; hence what is to be endured includes all the anxieties that attend the exercise of our agency. "Yes; . . . it is [God's] earth, and he controlleth according to his pleasure, and it will yet be devoted to those who serve him. But, in consequence of the agency that is given to the intelligent children of our Father and God, it is contrary to his laws, government, and character for him to dictate us in our actions any further than we prefer."[8]

This reality requires our making our way through and patiently enduring life's sometimes vexing choices, for in Father's plan not only is "there . . . an opposition in all things" (2 Nephi 2:11), but facts, said Brigham, are demonstrated by "their opposites," for "we find ourselves surrounded . . . by an almost endless combination of opposites, through which we must pass to gain experience and information to fit us for an eternal progression."[9]

Though the record in Brigham Young's Office Journal of 1857 is not complete, he apparently was asked a question which bears upon our need to endure it well: "Why are [we] left alone and often sad?" His response was that man has to learn to "act as an independent being . . . to see what he will do . . . to practice him . . . to be righteous in the dark—to be the friend of God."[10]

Brigham Young often counseled as to how our enduring is part of experiencing affliction personally, as in these words:

> It is like the words in the wind to talk about the sweetness of the honeycomb to those who have not tasted the opposite. You may talk about the glory and comfort of the light to those who never knew darkness, and what do they know about it? Nothing. You might as well preach to those lamps. If we can realize that everything in all the eternities that ever were and ever will be is ordained of God for the benefit and glory of intelligent beings, we can understand why he said to Joseph, "Against none is my anger kindled, only those who do not acknowledge my hand in all things." Do I acknowledge his hand? Yes. I told you in your afflictions, drivings, persecutions, and all that has been grievous to be borne, that the hand of God was in that as much as it was in bringing forth his revelations and the Priesthood through Joseph. . . . So with "Mormonism:" every time they give it a kick, it rises in the scale of power and influence in the world.[11]

Similarly, of criticism and persecution, President Gordon B. Hinckley has counseled us: "I conclude with this question: Should we be surprised if we are called upon to endure a little criticism, to make some small sacrifice for our faith, when our forebears paid so great a price for theirs?"[12]

Having personally observed much of the rising and falling of the tides of criticism, President Hinckley has reminded us of our present need to have the same wise perspective as that possessed by our predecessors:

> Joseph F. Smith presided over the Church at a time of great bit-terness toward our people. He was the target of vile accusations, of a veritable drumbeat of criticism by editorial writers even in this com-munity. He was lampooned, cartooned, and ridiculed. Listen to his response to those who made sport of demeaning him: "Let them alone. Let them go. Give them the liberty of speech they want. Let them tell their own story and write their own doom." . . . And then with an outreaching spirit of forgiving and forgetting, he went ahead with the great and positive work of leading the Church forward to new growth and remarkable accomplishments. At the time of his death, many of those who had ridiculed him wrote tributes of praise concerning him.[13]

Because living prophets are so precious a presence on the human scene, adversarial efforts to diminish and to mar them—past and present—should not be surprising. These men are thus called upon to endure efforts to "mar" them. The word *mar*, as used in certain scriptures, suggests to "spoil to a certain extent or to render less attractive," as if one were to mar furniture by scratching its surface but not harming its substance.

Isaiah speaks of the Lord's servant whose "visage" (or appear-ance) is marred (Isaiah 52:14). The resurrected Jesus speaks of a "great and marvelous work" which will not be believed by many, "although a man shall declare it unto them." This latter-day servant who was to bring Christ's word forth "shall be marred. . . . Yet . . . I will show unto them that my wisdom is greater than the cun-ning of the devil." (3 Nephi 21:9–10.) The Doctrine and Covenants (10:43) uses those same last words (about the wisdom of the Lord proving greater than the cunning of the devil) in reference to Joseph Smith and the coming forth of the Book of Mormon.

Joseph Smith, Sr., gave a father's blessing to the Prophet Joseph on 9 December 1834. In part of that blessing Father Smith quoted from ancient Joseph, who wondered how his latter-day posterity would receive the word of God. Then ancient Joseph's eyes beheld Joseph Smith, Jr., to be raised up in the last days. Ancient Joseph's soul was satisfied and he wept. Ancient Joseph was quoted by Father Smith as saying that the choice seer to arise "shall meditate great wisdom, [and his] intelligence shall circumscribe and comprehend the deep things of God, . . . though the wicked mar him for a little season."[14]

Church members should not be surprised, therefore, if enemies seek to "mar" prophets and the Presidents of the Church, or the Church itself, by seeming to render it, or us as members, less attractive and influential, thus causing some to turn away from or to discount the Lord's work and His servants. One of the early Twelve, Elder Orson Hyde, observed that the "shafts" intended for the Church "are always aimed at the head first."[15]

Being marred can be part of the experience of discipleship: "Blessed are ye, when men shall revile you, and persecute you, and shall say all manner of evil against you falsely, for my sake" (Matthew 5:11).

If we as members are likewise "marred" while doing the Lord's work, it will prove to be yet another dimension of sharing the fellowship of Christ's sufferings (see Philippians 3:10).

Prophets teach but also exemplify the way. Jacob, the poet-prophet, as have other prophets, also endured the challenge of not being heeded though having often testified and pleaded for repentance. Jesus' relevant lament surpassed all: "O Jerusalem, Jerusalem, thou that killest the prophets, and stonest them which are sent unto thee, how often would I have gathered thy children together, even as a hen gathereth her chickens under her wings, and ye would not!" (Matthew 23:37.)

Almost as if with a similar, resigned sigh, Jacob counseled, "O be wise: What can I say more? Finally, I bid you farewell, until I shall meet you before the pleasing bar of God." (Jacob 6:12–13.)

Prophets have a special appreciation, too, for Jacob's allegory of the olive trees. They can identify with the feelings of the Lord of the vineyard who, after all His labors, saw much evil fruit come forth. The twice-given lamentation of the Lord of the vineyard was: "What could I have done more for my vineyard?" (Jacob 5:41, 47.)

Paul told Timothy, his young brother in the gospel, "All scripture is given by inspiration of God, and is profitable for doctrine, . . . for instruction in righteousness" (2 Timothy 3:16). Obviously, all our canonized scriptures today, the Church's standard works, have come to us through men who at the time were living prophets to their people. These writings plus the inspired words of prophets of this dispensation, including those now living, constitute God's word to us.

In his day Alma found that the word of God in the scriptures and from living prophets had a "more powerful effect upon the minds of [his] people than "anything else" (Alma 31:5). In our day, "What can [they] say more?" (Jacob 6:12.) Our challenge is to be quick to draw upon the real power of special, prophetic words to help us, including those which can help us to endure well.

8

TRYING THE VIRTUE OF THE WORD OF GOD

When you understand the Gospel plan, you will comprehend that it is the most reasonable way of dealing with the human family (Brigham Young).[1]

We talk about our trials and troubles here in this life: but suppose that you could see yourselves thousands and millions of years after you have proved faithful to your religion during the few short years in this time, and have obtained eternal salvation and a crown of glory in the presence of God; then look back upon your lives here, and see the losses, crosses, and disappointments, the sorrows . . . you would be constrained to exclaim, "But what of all that? Those things were but for a moment, and we are now here. We have been faithful during a few moments in our mortality, and now we enjoy eternal life and glory, with power to progress in all the boundless knowledge and through the countless stages of progression, enjoying the smiles and approbation of our Father and God, and of Jesus Christ our elder brother." (Brigham Young.)[2]

Many times in human history the hopes of mankind have surged expectantly only to crash against the reefs of despair. Where for one reason or another there is ignorance of man's cosmic context and God's plans, hope wanes. Whether one is in search of peace or the end of disease and hunger, mortal plans and hopes tend to go awry. Alma found that "to lead [his] people" and to have a "powerful effect upon the minds of the people" the "word of God" was more powerful than "anything else" (Alma 31:5).

As often as not, when the passionate search for meaning is pursued along other paths it is muffled or simply overridden by demanding and consuming external events. Yet the quiet search for meaning continues like a vast and relentless river, sometimes roiling, sometimes meandering. When unrequited, however, the search for meaning carries away the unanchored topsoil of human hope. Thus in many places in the Lord's vineyard there remains no deepness of earth in which the gospel seed can grow. (See Matthew 13:5.)

Into this milieu came the Lord's "marvelous work and a wonder" (Isaiah 29:14). As likewise prophesied, however, the Restoration is also "strange work" by worldly standards (D&C 101:95; 95:4). Its revealed truths are simple and stunning. They bring meaning and identity to mankind—the very things for which so many mortals crave; for as the prophet foresaw, "they shall wander from sea to sea, and from the north even to the east, they shall run to and fro to seek the word of the Lord, and shall not find it" (Amos 8:12). The truth restored about life's purposes and man's identity can indeed, if accepted, prove to be "more powerful . . . than anything else."

Thus the Restoration is a latter-day rescue effort to nourish those who are parched, thirsty, and hungry—who need the living water and the bread of life but know not where to find it (see John 4:10–14); or, when they have found it, find themselves worrying needlessly over its "strangeness," or over the inexplicability of the Book of Mormon except for its having come forth by "the gift and power of God."

Granted, the Latter-day Saints may seem to be unlikely and "strange" repositories for something of such vast importance to mankind. But is the Restoration and its locus any more unlikely and "strange" than having the Atonement (for all mankind throughout all of history) accomplished in the meridian of time among the not so numerous Jewish people? The Lord did not choose ancient Israel because they were large in number: "The Lord did not set his love upon you, nor choose you, because ye were more in number than any people; for ye were the fewest of all people: but because the Lord loved you, and because he would keep the oath which he had sworn unto your fathers, hath the Lord brought you out with a mighty hand, and redeemed you out of the house of bondmen, from the hand of Pharaoh king of Egypt" (Deuteronomy 7:7–8).[3]

Paul in effect pointed out the irony of the situation that Jesus became a stumbling block to the Jews and foolishness to the Greeks (1 Corinthians 1:23). It was all simply too strange for most contemporaries back then even to consider and to take seriously.

No wonder the Lord used language indicating that as the work of the Restoration goes forward people will be given a chance to consider things they have "never considered" (D&C 101:94).

Meanwhile much of mankind, for the most part unknowingly, functions in the midst of doctrinal deprivation. True, the basic human yearnings are there, but these are covered over by the demanding daily cares of the world. When a few layers of preoccupation are peeled away, however, we see the waiting and even naked needs. An example of this is King Lamoni's father, who, statusful but sufficiently meek, spoke of his inner feelings in his first pleading to God (see Alma 22:18).

In the midst of wonderments over the vastness of space, Enoch's affirming declaration of God was, "Yet thou art there" (Moses 7:30). Man's search for meaning can be satisfied only with a knowledge of Heavenly Father and His plan. Even when the plan is known, however, it needs to be understood along with its implications. The world's doctrinal deprivation means that vast numbers of mortals remain tragically uninformed, like Laman and Lemuel, "who knew not the dealings of that God who had created them" (1 Nephi 2:12).

There are those who proudly insist that God jump through certain hoops and over certain hurdles in order to prove to them that He exists. Even if God were to condescend to do this, these individuals would badger Him in still other ways thereafter. There would be fresh demands, all symbolic of an inversion of roles. No wonder the first, great commandment is so specific! If it is not taken seriously, life will be lived very differently. Since many are offended at the idea of faith in God, another reason for the Restoration was "that faith also might increase in the earth" (D&C 1:21).

The preoccupations brought on by the daily cares of the world can be very demanding and consuming. There is the constant rush to satisfy the appetites of the natural man. The natural man (see Mosiah 3:19) is often fed but never filled. Even if his appetites are surfeited, his satisfactions are short-lived. The sense of emptiness relentlessly reappears. Even as gluttony digests its latest glob, it begins anticipating its next meal. The same pattern is there when it comes to the praise of men, or lust, or greed. Strange as it seems, the appetites of the natural man carry within themselves a capacity for the quick cancellation of any temporary satisfaction.

William Law said: "Now all trouble and uneasiness is founded in the want of something or other; would we therefore know the true cause of our troubles and disquiets, we must find out the cause of our wants; because that which creates, and increases our wants, does in the same degree create, and increase our trouble and disquiets. . . . The man of pride has a thousand wants, which only his own pride has created; and these render him as full of trouble, as if God had created him with a thousand appetites, without creating anything that was proper to satisfy them."[4]

These are among the reasons why Isaiah wrote: "But the wicked are like the troubled sea, when it cannot rest, whose waters cast up mire and dirt. There is no peace, saith my God, to the wicked." (Isaiah 57:20–21.)

Despite these appetites and their consequences, however—or sometimes perhaps as a result of them—some find their thoughts and feelings turning to spiritual things, like the quivering of some damaged but undying reflex left over from another place and another time. Though uncomprehended as to its meaning and implications, the yearning is there.

On the other hand, we who know the plan and the doctrines of the restored gospel are thus helped to draw upon "the virtue of the word of God." We lessen and even avoid murmuring or being "carried about with every wind of doctrine" (Ephesians 4:14).

The precious doctrines of the Restoration thus stand out, especially in a time when many "will not endure sound doctrine" (2 Timothy 4:3; see also Hebrews 13:9). So it is that we are expected, even required, to "teach one another the doctrine of the kingdom," which is "more powerful" than we sometimes realize (D&C 88:77).

In contrast to the richness of the Restoration, an anemic theology tends to produce weak faith. A partial doctrinal base cannot provide a fulness of faith. The less truth, the less firm and broad is conviction. The richness of the Restoration's theology, however, is capable of producing strong faith, including the faith to "endure it well."

It follows that we need to have a genuine and continuing intellectual involvement in order for us to move toward having "the mind of Christ" (1 Corinthians 2:16). After all, how could we worship with all our heart, might, *mind*, and strength without intellectual involvement? Time to ponder, to absorb, to serve, and to become even more the men and women of Christ—are all much needed. The gospel cannot strengthen us if we simply nibble at its edges occasionally, or if we are only marginally involved in worship and service.

God, who is a sharing and loving God, is anxious to teach us the weightier doctrines, "the deep things of God" (1 Corinthians 2:10). He has accelerated this imparting to us through the richness of the Restoration, which has been bestowed in what might be called the "Malachi measure": "there shall not be room enough to receive it" (Malachi 3:10; see also Matthew 23:23; 1 Corinthians 2:10). God's generosity could be expressed in this imagery-laden scripture: "And it shall be given unto you; good measure, pressed down, and shaken together, and running over" (Luke 6:38).

The Restoration's more complete doctrinal harvest is actually "running over." Moreover, it comes to us from God through prophets, prophet-editors, and prophet-translators. Fortunately, this is a protected process that guards against the dilutions and distortions of both men and time.

Let us consider a few illustrative examples of the comparative richness of the Restoration and how it enlarges and enhances our knowledge of fundamentals. We will inventory briefly, therefore, but a few restored truths about the universe, preexistence, Christ, the resurrection, God's plan of salvation, and the scriptures.

As we review these several doctrines, bear in mind President Young's caution that the restored gospel is not "comely." In fact, in its comparative strangeness it is a stumbling block to many. Hugh Nibley reminds us of how jarring certain of the restored doctrines are to some. Charles Dickens, the one who watched emigrants leaving the British harbor for America, interviewed some of them and described them as "the pick and flower of England." Even so, Dickens did not regard the religious movement's doctrines very highly, because "it exhibits fanaticism in its newest garb," "seeing visions in the age of railways."[5]

Granted, many mortals who are without the gospel's fulness do well with what light they have, and they display commendable faith. One reason is that all have originally been given the "light that lighteth every man that cometh into the world," and some have carefully nurtured and preserved that light (John 4:9; D&C 93:2). Still others are only "kept from the truth because they know not where to find it" (D&C 123:12). Moreover, many individuals instinctively have certain correct beliefs even though these may be excluded by their religion's formal theology.

The "headline" comparisons to follow are but a few indicators of the richness and relevancy of the Restoration as compared with the views of some disbelievers and some believers—representative of those not blessed with the Restoration.

First, let us consider illustrative views of the universe. Some disbelievers regard the universe as "godless geometric space." Some see man as being hopelessly situated in "an unsponsored universe," a universe "without a master," which "cares nothing for [man's] hopes and fears," an "empire of chance" in which man falls victim to "the trampling march of unconscious power."[6]

Many who believe the Bible, in contrast, warmly acknowledge the following words of Isaiah—though not all of their implications: "For thus saith the Lord that created the heavens; God himself that formed the earth and made it; he hath established it, he created it not in vain, he formed it to be inhabited" (Isaiah 45:18).

These same believers may also acknowledge the words of Paul, that God "hath in these last days spoken unto us by his Son, whom he hath appointed heir of all things, by whom also he made the worlds" (Hebrews 1:2). Bereft of the Restoration, however, these believers may stumble over the doctrine of the plurality of worlds; they often end up believing, by implication at least, in a God who is a one-planet-God; who is "there," but often seems detached, His plans and purposes not being easily or clearly known to mankind except by revelation.

With the Restoration, however, comes greater fulness. This includes, of course, the biblical views such as those of Isaiah and Paul. But these are measurably "added upon" as we learn more of God's clear purposes. "For behold, this is my work and my glory—to bring to pass the immortality and eternal life of man" (Moses 1:39). How vast are God's dominions? "And worlds without number have I created; and I also created them for mine own purpose; and by the Son I created them" (Moses 1:33).

By whom were they created? "And by the Son I created them,

which is mine Only Begotten" (Moses 1:33). "That by [Christ,] and through him, and of him, the worlds are and were created, and the inhabitants thereof are begotten sons and daughters unto God" (D&C 76:24). "The heavens . . . are many, and they cannot be numbered unto man, but they are numbered unto me, for they are mine" (Moses 1:37).

The Restoration gives us few details concerning the universe, of course, but from what we are given we know that we are not alone, and that we are in the midst of meaning and of unfolding, divine purposes.

Though understandably desiring to know more, we do not presently possess the capacity to absorb more. Nor do we have an adequate "security clearance." This was the case with Moses: "But only an account of this earth, and the inhabitants thereof, give I unto you. For behold, there are many worlds that have passed away by the word of my power. And there are many that now stand, and innumerable are they unto man; but all things are numbered unto me, for they are mine and I know them." (Moses 1:35.)

Physicist Paul Horowitz of Harvard University is paraphrased as saying that "if the recent discovery of a planet circling a nearby star is a normal, mundane consequence of the ordinary star-making process, it is likely that millions of stars within our own Milky Way galaxy have Earthlike planets."[7] Enoch, we remember, in speaking of God's creations, mentioned "millions of earths like this" (Moses 7:30).

Another of the most stunning and explanatory revelations restored through the Restoration is the doctrine of premortal existence. But mortal views of premortality, once again, vary widely. Non-believers deny that man had any premortality; instead, to them he is a creature who was formed by unconscious power and who is doomed to perish. Still others, however, like Marcel Proust, apparently have had momentary wonderments even amid their general disbeliefs. "Everything is arranged in this life as though we entered it carrying the burden of obligations contracted in a former life; . . . obligations which . . . seem to belong to a different world, founded upon kindness, . . . which we leave in order to be born into this world."[8]

Many Christians clearly and gratefully believe God created man, all right, but that He did so *ex nihilo*—"out of nothing"—

thus ruling out any premortal personality or individual identity. Other believers are well represented by the articulate and faith-filled views of those like J.R.R. Tolkien, who wrote:

> Dis-graced [man] may be, yet is not dethroned,
> and keeps the rags of lordship once he owned.[9]

After the deaths of the Apostles, and before the doctrine of premortality was lost to apostasy, a few early Christian fathers, such as the two to follow, nevertheless understood certain things: "If men by their good works prove themselves to be worthy of His plan, they are considered qualified, we take it, to return to His presence and to rule with Him."[10]

And from Clement: "Let us consider therefore, brethren, whereof we are made; who, and what kind of men we came into the world, . . . [God] that made us, and formed us, brought us into his own world; having presented us with his benefits, even before we were born." [11]

With the Restoration, however, we are blessed to understand that individual intelligences were organized before the world was (see Abraham 3:22; see also D&C 138). "Man was also in the beginning with God," and thus man is co-eternal, but certainly not co-equal, with God (see Abraham 3:18, 19; D&C 93:23, 29). The foreordination of some, based on God's foreknowledge, was and is a reality.

> Before I formed thee in the belly I knew thee; and before thou camest forth out of the womb I sanctified thee, and I ordained thee a prophet unto the nations (Jeremiah 1:5; see also Ecclesiastes 12:7; John 9:2; Ephesians 1:4; Hebrews 12:9).

> And this is the manner after which they were ordained—being called and prepared from the foundation of the world according to the foreknowledge of God (Alma 13:3).

> Among the great and mighty ones who were assembled in this vast congregation of the righteous were Father Adam, the Ancient of Days and father of all,
> And our glorious Mother Eve, with many of her faithful daughters who had lived through the ages and worshiped the true and living God (D&C 138:38-39).

The lyrics in the hymn "I Am a Child of God" contain reflections of the revelations concerning our premortal existence and the purposes of mortal life.

> I am a child of God,
> And he has sent me here,
> Has given me an earthly home
> With parents kind and dear.
>
> I am a child of God,
> And so my needs are great;
> Help me to understand his words
> Before it grows too late.
>
> I am a child of God.
> Rich blessings are in store;
> If I but learn to do his will
> I'll live with him once more.
>
> *Chorus:*
> Lead me, guide me, walk beside me,
> Help me find the way.
> Teach me all that I must do
> To live with him some-day.

As to the divine purposes of mortal life and the reality of the subsequent resurrection, disbelievers of course do not credit such views at all. Those who despair of meaning and immortality are represented in these quotations: "Are all men's lives . . . broken, tumultuous, agonized and unromantic, punctuated by screams, imbecilities, agonies and death? Who knows? . . . I don't know. . . . Why can't people have what they want? The things were all there to content everybody, yet everybody got the wrong thing. I don't know. It's beyond me. It's all darkness."[12]

And again: Mankind is "destined to extinction. . . . There is nothing we can do." "We have no personal life beyond the grave. There is no God. Fate knows nor wrath nor ruth."[13]

"When a man was dead, that was the end thereof" (Alma 30:18).

Undernourished near-believers may have the toughest time. Afflicted with ambivalence, some wander to and fro upon the earth in search of truth without knowing where to find it (see Amos 8:11–12; D&C 123:12). One such prominent wanderer was described by a colleague: "It is strange how he persists . . . in wandering to-and-fro. . . . He can neither believe, nor be comfortable in his unbelief."[14]

Without knowing the plan of salvation some believers struggle to find the meaning and purpose of life—as in this candid, sincere, but sad expression: "All of my life I have struggled to find the purpose of living. I have tried to answer three questions which always seemed to be fundamental: the problem of eternity; the problems of human personality; and the problems of evil. I have failed. I have solved none of them . . . and I believe no one will ever solve them."[15]

Without a knowledge of premortality and God's plan of salvation, arriving at an accurate theodicy is difficult. Some wonder poignantly, If God is all-good and all-powerful, why does He permit so much suffering and evil in this world He created? The special contribution to theodicy made by the Restoration has yet to be set forth by a full demonstration of its unusual richness, though we touch upon this relevant matter frequently.

Moving on to mankind's future, many have a sincere, generalized faith in some sort of resurrection. This view, widely held, is movingly epitomized by the touching epitaph at Corregidor anticipating that those who fell there in battle will one day be resurrected, when they "hear the low, clear reveille of God."

Once again, the Restoration brings a striking and needed enlargement of view concerning the purposes of mortal life, including the reality of the resurrection: "This is my work and my glory—to bring to pass the immortality and eternal life of man" (Moses 1:39); "Men are, that they might have joy" (2 Nephi 2:25).

The resurrection is real and ongoing and will be inclusive:

Many saints did arise and appear unto many and did minister unto them (3 Nephi 23:11).

And the graves were opened; and many bodies of the saints which slept arose, and came out of the graves after his resurrection, and went into the holy city, and appeared unto many (Matthew 27:52–53; see also 3 Nephi 23:7–12).

> And I saw the dead, small and great, stand before God; and the books were opened: and another book was opened, which is the book of life: and the dead were judged out of those things which were written in the books, according to their works (Revelation 20:12).

Bearing testimony of the centrality and reality of the resurrection is a significant part of the duties laid upon us by the Restoration. "And righteousness will I send down out of heaven; and truth will I send forth out of the earth, to bear testimony of mine Only Begotten; his resurrection from the dead; yea, and also the resurrection of all men; and righteousness and truth will I cause to sweep the earth as with a flood" (Moses 7:62).

Likewise articulated is the portion and place of the spirit world in Heavenly Father's plan of salvation.

> And there were gathered together in one place an innumerable company of the spirits of the just, who had been faithful in the testimony of Jesus while they lived in mortality;
> And who had offered sacrifice in the similitude of the great sacrifice of the Son of God, and had suffered tribulation in their Redeemer's name.
> All these had departed the mortal life, firm in the hope of a glorious resurrection, through the grace of God the Father and his Only Begotten Son, Jesus Christ.
> I beheld that they were filled with joy and gladness, and were rejoicing together because the day of their deliverance was at hand.
> They were assembled awaiting the advent of the Son of God into the spirit world, to declare their redemption from the bands of death. (D&C 138:12–16.)

God has a plan of happiness and salvation. One of the great purposes of the Restoration was to bring back not only knowledge of that plan but also the precious process of revelation for conveying that and other priceless knowledge.

> And after God had appointed that these things should come unto man, behold, then he saw that it was expedient that man should know concerning the things whereof he had appointed unto them;

Therefore he sent angels to converse with them, who caused men to behold of his glory.

And they began from that time forth to call on his name; therefore God conversed with men, and made known unto them the plan of redemption, which had been prepared from the foundation of the world; and this he made known unto them according to their faith and repentance and their holy works. (Alma 12:28–30.)

The above is precisely the process utilized in the Restoration. Note how central to God's purposes communicating about His plan of salvation is. "And the great God has had mercy on us, and made these things known unto us that we might not perish; yea, and he has made these things known unto us beforehand, because he loveth our souls as well as he loveth our children; therefore, in his mercy he doth visit us by his angels, that the plan of salvation might be made known unto us as well as unto future generations" (Alma 24:14).

Regarding the various views mortals hold about Jesus Christ, disbelievers and near-believers simply do not accept Him as mankind's great Redeemer. Some of these individuals see Jesus as an admirable but passing moral teacher who was confined to a small geographic space and a very brief period of history. Jesus ends up in their view as a very good man. But not as a redeeming God! Moreover, since others were crucified in that period of time, Christ's crucifixion occupies no special place in their scheme of things. Hence these individuals deny the Lord "that bought them" (2 Peter 2:1).

Some regard Jesus, again at best, as one of the greatest prophets but do not fully understand His identity. Other unsettled believers worry needlessly because the secular historicity of Jesus is not firm; this concerns them unduly, lacking, as they do, the reaffirming richness of the Restoration.

Many believers, on the other hand, truly and sincerely worship Jesus while incorrectly viewing Him as being both the Father and the Son. Similarly, many faithfully expect some kind of reappearance of Jesus ushering in a millennial reign.

With the Restoration, however, we Latter-day Saints are blessed to understand much more regarding the roles and identity of Jesus. Jesus is the firstborn spirit child of the Father, the Only

Begotten in the flesh, the creating Lord of the universe, and the great shepherd of this planet (see D&C 20:21; 76:24; Colossians 1:15; Hebrews 13:20).

Jesus was sent by the Father to be the Redeemer of all mankind, making possible the resurrection of all mankind, the essence of Christ's gospel (3 Nephi 27:13–16; D&C 76:40–42). Jesus, as John wrote, "increased in wisdom and stature, and in favour with God and man" (Luke 2:52). "And I, John, saw that he received not of the fulness at the first, but received grace for grace; and he received not of the fulness at first, but continued from grace to grace, until he received a fulness; and thus he was called the Son of God, because he received not of the fulness at the first" (D&C 93:12–14). Yet He "needed not that any man should teach Him" (JST Matthew 3:25).

Jesus is thus the Lord of all the prophets, not merely one of them. He was the Jehovah of the Old Testament prior to coming as a babe to Bethlehem to serve humanity as the Mortal Messiah. "Thus saith the Lord your God, even Jesus Christ, the Great I Am, Alpha and Omega, the beginning and the end, the same which looked upon the wide expanse of eternity, and all the seraphic hosts of heaven, before the world was made" (D&C 38:1).

This co-identity—Jehovah and Jesus—was well known by earlier prophets: "We knew of Christ . . . many hundred years before his coming" (Jacob 4:4; see also 3 Nephi 15:5; D&C 110:3–4). Moses, like Jacob, similarly understood, for Paul observed that Moses "esteem[ed] the reproach of Christ greater riches than the treasures in Egypt" (Hebrews 11:26).

Having passed through mortality and having overcome the world, Jesus became perfect even as the Father is perfect (see 3 Nephi 12:48; 27:27; see also Matthew 5:48).

Christ will come again in majesty and power. It is striking to compare the anticipatory and prophetic, but sparse, words of Zechariah with the fulness of those in Section 45 of the Doctrine and Covenants: "And one shall say unto him, What are these wounds in thine hands? Then he shall answer, Those with which I was wounded in the house of my friends." (Zechariah 13:6.) "And then shall the Jews look upon me and say: What are these wounds in thine hands and in thy feet? Then shall they know that I am the Lord; for I will say unto them: These wounds are the wounds with which I was wounded in the house of my friends. I am he who was lifted up. I am Jesus that was crucified. I am the Son of God." (D&C 45:51–52.)

No wonder we are still inventorying the harvest basket of the Restoration! Having dashed about the wonder-filled landscape of the Restoration, exclaiming and observing, we should not be surprised if some of our first impressions prove to be more childish than definitive. Brushing against such tall timber, we have the scent of pine inevitably upon us. Our pockets are stuffed with souvenir cones and colorful rocks, and we are filled with childish glee. There is no way to grasp it all. Little wonder that some of us mistake a particular tree for the whole of the forest, or that in our exclamations there are some unintended exaggerations. We have seen far too much to describe. We "cannot say the smallest part which [we] feel" (Alma 26:16).

No matter! Further familiarization and exploration will increase not only our understanding but also our wonder. After all, He who is not given to hyperbole used the words "marvelous work and a wonder" to describe it all. (See Isaiah 29:14; D&C 4:1; 1 Nephi 22:8.)

Following our initial discovering and exclaiming, a deep appreciation and a hushed expectancy settle in. We are realizing that "the day cometh that . . . all things shall be revealed unto the children of men which ever have been among the children of men, and which ever will be even unto the end of the earth" (2 Nephi 27:11).

What is yet to come will further expand our "views of Christ" and will enlarge our understanding of the resurrection and all that is central to Heavenly Father's plan of salvation.

Having thus briefly compared the Restoration's fulness, we should remember that God sometimes gives "a lesser part" "to try their faith" (3 Nephi 26:8, 9; see also Jacob 4:14). If it is received, more is given; if not, "then shall the greater things be withheld," for "I will try the faith of my people" (vv. 10, 11). Faith is central; hence even the Apostles pleaded, "Lord, increase our faith" (Luke 17:5).

Does this divine withholding occur in order to demonstrate, again and again, that we cannot make our way through the mortal maze, unless we submit to the Lord? For those who have not had the experience, being in a real, physical maze would make one wish for directive help from one with a view from above. The only way through the mortal maze has been thus pointed out.

Is it too much otherwise to expect mortals to have such perspective? Yes, it is if we are left to ourselves to endure. Being real brothers and sisters in communities of Saints while in mortality helps greatly, however, even crucially, as we "strengthen" each other. The truly converted will not be diverted from their duties to God or to each other.

9

LIVING IN A COMMUNITY OF SAINTS

Again, the kingdom of heaven is like unto a net, that was cast into the sea, and gathered of every kind (Matthew 13:47).

The Lord had a perfect Church, then He let all of us come inside. (The late Dr. Henry Eyring, faithful disciple and eminent scientist.)

And it came to pass that I, Nephi, beheld the power of the Lamb of God, that it descended upon the saints of the church of the Lamb, and upon the covenant people of the Lord, who were scattered upon all the face of the earth; and they were armed with righteousness and with the power of God in great glory (1 Nephi 14:14).

In the last days, even with significant Church growth, human wickedness will set limits on the growth of the kingdom (see 1 Nephi 14:12). At the same time, God's disciples will achieve unity amid diversity and will be "armed with righteousness" (v. 14). The glory of God will eventually rest in great power upon His sanctified people, even given the side-by-side, "wheat and tares" circumstances (see D&C 105:32; Matthew 13:24–30).

Being in communities of Saints is made even more essential by the sharp decline of traditional communities, at least in much of the world. The current trends, including those noted in chapters 2 and 3, reflect more and more functional as well as affectional separations of citizens, including depersonalized urban living. Alas, it is regrettable that those who live in neighborhoods are not necessarily neighbors.

Today's separation results not only from a loss of community but also from the increasingly profound segmentation and specialization of modern life: we care less, know less of each other, and have less in common as neighbors.

Americans need to be wary of the nation's declining social capital, the bank of trust formed from engagements in the shared service of its citizens in various associations. Of all these associations, wrote Robert Putnam, the family and religious affiliations are the most common and contributive. But there are other contributors like PTAs, women's clubs, the Red Cross, Boy Scouts, Girl Scouts, fraternal organizations, and so forth.[1]

Participation in many of these organizations, however, has been eroding and shrinking in America. Furthermore, instead of these interactive and overlapping networks, we now see more and more single-interest and single-issue pressure groups.

Meanwhile technology, a blessing in a great many respects, nevertheless can divide and make us even more solitary souls. Television, for instance, observed Robert D. Putnam, "has made our communities . . . wider and shallower."[2] The recurring irony of some talk shows is illustrative. These often feature those who bare their inmost souls to strangers but cannot converse effectively with spouse or children!

Long ago, de Tocqueville anticipated what American individualism, unenriched by family and community, could produce: "Thus, not only does democracy make every man forget his ancestors, but it hides his descendants and separates his contemporaries from him; it throws him back forever upon himself alone, and threatens in the end to confine him entirely within the solitude of his own heart."[3] One outcome has been called "the lonely crowd."

Errant individualism further adds to the slackness regarding community, with every man "walking in his own way, and after the image of his own god . . . in the likeness of the world," resembling circumstances anciently when "there was no king in Israel [and] every man did that which was right in his own eyes." (D&C 1:16; Judges 21:25.)

Information highways can bring many blessings, but insofar as their promised capactiy to connect us is concerned, they may end up cutting an even wider swath through more traditional families and communities. Individuals may be drenched with information while being isolated even more from association with real people right around them and from real conversations with those living next door. Traveling the information highway is no substitute for walking the straight and narrow path. Being saturated with data even brings to mind a prophecy about those who are "ever learning, and never able to come to the knowledge of the truth" (2 Timothy 3:7). Megabytes, however large and helpful, are no substitute for partaking of the bread of life.

Thus living in an age which celebrates errant individualism at the expense of community, we can better endure it well if we are not only members of the living Church but also, within that larger fold, we belong to a community of Saints. In a community of Saints—clusters of faithful families, neighborhoods, branches, and wards who are "alive in Christ"—we are greatly supported as we strive to live "in" but to not be "of" the world.

The best single description of such a community of Saints is captured in this account:

> And it came to pass that he said unto them: Behold, here are the waters of Mormon (for thus were they called) and now, as ye are desirous to come into the fold of God, and to be called his people, and are willing to bear one another's burdens, that they may be light;
>
> Yea, and are willing to mourn with those that mourn; yea, and comfort those that stand in need of comfort, and to stand as witnesses of God at all times and in all things, and in all places that ye may be in, even until death, that ye may be redeemed of God, and be numbered with those of the first resurrection, that ye may have eternal life. . . .

In fact, being assimilated into such a community or fold should precede, as well as follow, joining the Church formally, for,

> . . . if this be the desire of your hearts, what have you against being baptized in the name of the Lord, as a witness before him that ye have entered into a covenant with him, that ye will serve him and keep his commandments, that he may pour out his Spirit more abundantly upon you?
>
> And now when the people had heard these words, they clapped their hands for joy, and exclaimed: This is the desire of our hearts. (Mosiah 18:8–11.)

Preparation for Church membership is to be anything but casual, and enduring therein is not to be accomplished in isolation: "And again, by way of commandment to the church concerning the manner of baptism—All those who humble themselves before God, and desire to be baptized, and come forth with broken hearts and contrite spirits, and witness before the church that they have truly repented of all their sins, and are willing to take upon them the name of Jesus Christ, having a determination to serve him to the end, and truly manifest by their works that they have received of the Spirit of Christ unto the remission of their sins, shall be received by baptism into his church (D&C 20:37).

It is abundantly clear, therefore, that we have a duty to comfort others, to mourn with them, to serve them, and to help them. When there is so much to do to help others, there is little time for self-pity. We do not know all the details of the crosses others bear, but we know enough to understand that crosses are being borne valiantly. Moreover, the courage of others can be contagious.

During our mortal schooling in submissiveness we will see the visible crosses that some carry, but other crosses will go unseen and unappreciated. A few individuals may appear to have no trials at all—which, if it were so, would be a trial in itself. If, as do trees, our souls had rings to measure the years of greatest personal growth, the wide rings would likely reflect the years of greatest moisture—but from tears, not rainfall.

Ordinances and associations converge in communities of Saints: "It is expedient that the church meet together often to partake of bread and wine in the remembrance of the Lord Jesus" (D&C 20:75), "Thou shalt live together in love, insomuch that thou shalt weep for the loss of them that die, and more especially for those that have not hope of a glorious resurrection" (D&C 42:45).

Even while giving much to others in need in such communities, we must also be meek enough to learn how blessed it is to receive from the ministrations of others.

The disciples' inquiry about the blind man (whether it was he or his parents that had sinned) called forth Jesus' stunning response (see John 9:2–3). Jesus indicated that neither the blind man nor his parents had sinned; rather, the man was in that condition "that the works of God should be made manifest in him." These "works of God" are seen not only in healings but in the enduring shown in the lives of people who become walking witnesses to the mercy and power of God. These individuals in one way or another become portable and observable sermons, as "the works of God" are "manifest in [them]."

Exemplifying neighbors are a great blessing in many ways. So are congregations where, when an especially spiritual sacrament meeting is over, one sees a lingering of caring members that is not unlike the lingering of those who were overcome after Jesus had taught and blessed people (see 3 Nephi 17:18).

The rest of us thus are blessed to associate with remarkable individuals who are in the process of enduring trials. The Lord has told us He has "designs" which are related to our enduring certain tribulations (see D&C 58:3). "For the present time," however, faith is needed, since we are not always able to see all "the design" of our God nor "the glory which shall follow." The latter is a hard but very reassuring doctrine; and it is measurably softened when we are among practicing and exemplifying believers.

We are sometimes called upon especially to serve as "secondary sufferers." In some respects, secondary sufferers often have a tougher time than the primary sufferers. Many secondary sufferers also endure it well in meeting the particular challenges they face. They honor the endurance of the primary sufferer by displaying grace and courage in the midst of "all these things." More than a few husbands and wives almost seem to take turns, rotating roles as primary and secondary sufferers as a spouse just emerging from a medical crisis is now called upon to nurse the other, again.

In communities of Saints we actually witness more lessons than we can absorb, including how varied trials can be. A friend of mine who had known a special trial meekly said, "If it's fair, it's not a trial." If something were "fair," there would be one less grievance to endure. Likewise, if something were "fair" in terms of its timing, at least there could be no complaint over the Lord's calendaring. Fair or unfair, however, it helps to be comforted by fellow disciples when we stand in need of comfort in trying times (see Mosiah 18:9).

Empathy and exemplification are all about us—to instruct us, to inspire us, and to reassure us.

Maintaining individual equipoise is likewise less difficult when we are part of such balanced communities of Saints. Otherwise we are much more alone, being unrelievedly "encompassed . . . round about" by the "natural man" *en masse* (see D&C 76:29). Without the gospel, mortals are viewed very pessimistically by some: "In human nature, generous impulses are occasional or reversible. They are spent in childhood, in dreams, in extremities, and they are often weak or soured in old age. They form amiable interludes like tearful sentiments in a ruffian, or they are pleasant self-deceptive hypocrisies acted out, like civility to strangers, because such is in society the path of least resistance. Strain the situation, however, dig a little beneath the surface, and you will find a ferocious, persistent, profoundly selfish man."[4]

If we are not careful and correctly informed about the true identity of others, it is easy to despair and to stereotype. Stereotyping reflects both intellectual laziness and lovelessness. The straight and narrow path leads us to a wide horizon of discovering and knowing people, but stereotyping confines us in the solitude of a conceptual cul-de-sac.

It is not surprising that other observers find exemplars with characteristics resembling those in communities of Saints.

> Many of our exemplars found in their faiths a seemingly boundless capacity for forgiveness and charity—a capacity that lay at the heart of their moral activities. In fact, it is hard to imagine how the exemplars could have overcome the dispiriting frustrations of their work, such as betrayal and ingratitude from those whom they served, without such a capacity. Exemplars who exhibited the capacity of forgiveness and charity avoided the bitterness and negativity of the few who did not. Most often, this capacity was firmly rooted in a spiritual faith, a belief in God, a transcendent force for the good.[5]

What, however, of our responsibilities to those beyond our communities of Saints? Church members should be good neighbors to all, cooperating with others regarding shared concerns in larger communities. This can be done, if we are thoughtful, without subordinating gospel principles or our spiritual integrity. As members do things for the best of reasons, we will build up a supply of good will that will stand us in good stead should we later differ with others on matters of doctrine.

It is significant that the Church itself is instructed to stand "independent above all [that is] beneath the celestial world" (D&C 78:14). This does not mean aloofness, however. Rather, this permits cooperation in a "good cause" with appropriate sensitivity to diversity. Clearly the Church must neither allow its doctrines to be diluted nor its people to be diminished by compromising with the ways of the world. Yet the second great commandment is not to be applied solely to one's immediate ingroup.

There is also a related risk: bending too much to accommodate local cultures or to do what is, for the moment, politically and culturally correct. "Nevertheless among the chief rulers also many believed on him; but because of the Pharisees they did not confess him, lest they should be put out of the synagogue: for they loved the praise of men more than the praise of God" (John 12:42–43). But where is that particular synagogue now? Where, too, are those Pharisees—of whom some near converts were so afraid in the midst of a sharp "division among the people"? (See John 7:43–48.) The Pharisees, as a movement, actually lasted only a relatively short span of time and then faded into history.

Though required to be good citizens, we must not become inordinately attached to nations, either. Not only are we to be headed for a celestial culture, but the millennial time will come when the Lord will "[make] a full end of all nations" (D&C 87:6).

Meanwhile, local and national cultures can have a profound influence upon us. But we are headed for a celestial culture. This everlasting culture was previewed for us in connection with the unique city of Enoch and also among the Church members in the Americas after the resurrected Jesus departed (see Moses 7:18; 4 Nephi 1:17). The characteristics noted included being "in one, the children of Christ," but with no social and economic subdivisions, no "ites" and no "isms." The outcomes are joyous to contemplate:

> And it came to pass that there was no contention in the land, because of the love of God which did dwell in the hearts of the people.
>
> And there were no envyings, nor strifes, nor tumults, nor whoredoms, nor lyings, nor murders, nor any manner of lasciviousness; and surely there could not be a happier people among all the people who had been created by the hand of God.
>
> There were no robbers, nor murderers, neither were there Lamanites, nor any manner of -ites; but they were in one, the children of Christ, and heirs to the kingdom of God. (4 Nephi 1:15–17.)

Later, however, there began to be subdivisions once again among the Nephites, hence multiple troubles also began to arise again in the land. Many resumed the follies that previously had brought so much misery.

Thus the relevancy of "love thy neighbor," if practiced successfully "here and now," one day will demonstrate how it will be applied in the coming "there and then"—in a neighborhood as wide as the universe!

Given their importance, how can we better facilitate in the here and now the building of these communities of Saints, those human-sized clusters of families, neighborhoods, branches, and wards?

First, shepherds of the flock and members of a community of Saints should know the doctrines of and how to administer the kingdom: "And now, behold, I give unto you a commandment, that when ye are assembled together ye shall instruct and edify each other, that ye may know how to act and direct my church, how to act upon the points of my law and commandments, which I have given" (D&C 43:8).

Shepherds are thus to teach the doctrines and the correct principles of the kingdom to members, thus fixing accountability on the individual members of the community, lest they depart therefrom unadmonished and uninstructed.

A true community of Saints will also have a high ratio of those who are meek, being low demanders and high performers. However, efforts to build such communities will not succeed in a day, but, rather, "in process of time" (see Moses 7:21).

By associating together and sharing the needed experiences, we will get much practice, for instance, in meeting one of life's vexing challenges: to enlarge our compassion for those who are swollen with self-pity. This will include learning how difficult it is to pat a porcupine. We will also learn to weep together. In the grammar of the gospel, tears are like a quiet exclamation point punctuating poignancy.

Some in the Church have hands that hang down, no longer even expecting to be reached for. The imagery suggests those who have given up (see D&C 81:5). Learning to reach out and to "lift up" those particular hands is a vital part of life in the kingdom.

Other afflictions and unredeeming human tendencies are amply represented, for the gospel "net [gathereth] of every kind"

(Matthew 13:47). In such communities we even come to love those we don't even like initially.

We can learn something else together too, something having to do with duties and commitments. Brigham Young said of our sometimes inordinate attachment to material things and the comforts of life: "Some do not understand duties which do not coincide with their natural feelings and affections. Do you comprehend that statement? . . . There are duties which are above affection."[6] The various calls to duty give us chances to rise above mere pleasantry to contemplate the things of eternity.

There is thus ample clinical material within the communities of Saints to train us. There are, for instance, a few men in the Church who boast about how they hold the priesthood, while they are actually in the grip of their own egos.

We soon learn, too, while experiencing the rotations of leadership roles that are inevitable in the kingdom, that to be uncalled does not mean one is unworthy, unable, or unserviceable. Life in the Church means experiencing a variety of leaders not all of whom are always wise, mature, and deft. In fact, some of us are as bumpy and uneven as a sackful of old doorknobs. Some of the polishing we experience is actually a result of grinding against each other. How vital patience and lubricating love are in such circumstances!

Enduring likewise utilizes our patience and meekness when, for the moment, we have more to offer to the kingdom than there seem to be chances to give and to contribute. The gears as between what is offered, on the one hand, and the gears of opportunity to utilize these talents and gifts, on the other hand, are not perfectly matched. These frustrations can be real, especially for those who may for the moment feel underwhelmed.

While though those particular gears may not always match, there is certainly no such problem of being underwhelmed in daily life as regards opportunities to honor our covenants and keep the commandments. There is never anything underwhelming about those challenges! It is important, therefore, to differentiate between the occasional frustrations resulting from unmatched gears and the pervasive reality that none of us can complain that we are being underused or under-tested when it comes to keeping our covenants or the commandments.

Paul's teachings on the interdependency of Church members

are particularly relevant to the building of these special communities. Amid our diverse talents, backgrounds, and personalities, the eye cannot say to the hand, "I have no need of thee" (1 Corinthians 12:21). The concert pianist cannot say to the lowly piano tuner, "I have no need of thee." The pianist's great music would not be possible on an untuned piano. Correspondingly, the tuner is unlikely to be able to play the piano superbly. Both use their hands, however, to the edification of all. So it is in a true community of Saints, where there "are diversities of gifts, but the same Spirit" (1 Corinthians 12:4).

Often missing in human relationships in the world but present in these special communities is corrective but loving commentary. Members are to edify and serve one another, and the Church is to admonish individual members as needed. This is part of the perfecting process. (See Mosiah 26:6.)

Admonition is not always well received, of course. In reproving members at Galatia, Paul wrote, rhetorically, "Am I therefore become your enemy, because I tell you the truth?" (Galatians 4:16.) Not even those the Church reproved were to be counted as enemies (see 2 Thessalonians 3:15).

Can we endure well corrective counsel even in such communities? The Prophet Joseph taught, "When a corrupt man is chastised he gets angry and will not endure it."[7] Joseph and other valiants endured well having their occasional chastisements from the Lord, including having these set forth publicly for all to see. The world is often either too cruel in correction or abstains altogether therefrom. For us, "speaking the truth in love" (Ephesians 4:15) and showing forth "an increase of love" (D&C 121:43) make all the difference.

Enduring involves coping successfully with customized chastening. "If ye endure chastening, God dealeth with you as with sons; for what son is he whom the father chasteneth not? . . . Now no chastening for the present seemeth to be joyous, but grievous: nevertheless afterward it yieldeth the peaceable fruit of righteousness unto them which are exercised thereby." (Hebrews 12:7, 11.)

Members who speak the truth in love help each other in many ways. One way is helping each other to endure it well. Giving neighborly admonitions is better than creating self-serving media events, anyway, for the latter only serve to create or to perpetuate adversarial relationships. Therefore, Jesus' prescription should be lovingly and generously applied: "Moreover if thy brother shall trespass against thee, go and tell him his fault between thee and him alone: if he shall hear thee, thou hast gained thy brother" (Matthew 18:15).

We have many opportunities to balance giving needed admonition with the needed sensitivity urged by Paul—that we be especially forgiving of the admonished, lest he be "swallowed up with overmuch sorrow" (1 Corinthians 2:7). Once again, the Lord's further direction is to show "forth afterwards an increase of love" (D&C 121:43).

There are, however, those among us who would rather try to change the Church than to change themselves. Such individuals either are ignorant of or choose to ignore a fundamental fact concerning the kingdom of God: that it is not a democracy, it is a kingdom. The law of common consent is a significant check and balance, but the Church is still a kingdom. Those who would want to liken the Church to their own image do not realize how ludicrous, even if it were possible, doing this would be. Walking our own way creates its own ironies and "should warm every atheist's heart. For if God is a socially conscious political being whose views invariably correspond to our own prejudices on every essential point of doctrine, he demands of us no more than our politics require. . . . [H]ow would our worship of [this kind of being] constitute more than self-congratulation for our own moral standards? As an atheist, I like this God. It is good to see him every morning while I am shaving."[8]

Besides, why would any one want to belong to a Church which could be readily changed to resemble him? As members, we are to strive to resemble Jesus, after whom the Church is named, and to seek to have His image in our countenances (3 Nephi 27:27; Alma 5:14). Those whose primary purpose is to be a self-centered and recruiting change agent should recall Groucho Marx's relevant line about his not wanting to belong to any club that would have him as a member!

The doctrines are God's, not ours. His power is His to delegate, not ours to manipulate. Those who want to shape and remake things to their own liking have ample opportunities to do so by establishing their own secular organizations. For us, the goal is clearly to make God's work our own—not the other way around. Those in communities of Saints understand this reality.

Even so, communities of Saints are also quick to reach out to their members, including those who, consciously or otherwise, try running away from God. But God, who has created worlds without number, still notices the fall of every sparrow. He even advises us that the hairs of our heads are numbered (see Matthew 10:29, 30). Actually, runaways cannot even make it off the porch unnoticed, let alone down the road, before God's arm reaches out to them, often through utilizing visiting teachers or home teachers or leaders. God's reassurance is that "mine arm is lengthened out all the day long" (2 Nephi 28:32). Such should likewise be the redeeming posture of those in communities of saints toward all members. Of none should it ever be said "I have no need of thee" (1 Corinthians 12:21).

Besides, the returning prodigals report poignantly and constantly that it is impossible to run away from God's love or beyond His reach. He stands "with open arms to receive" the repentant (Mormon 6:17). The repentant will, one day, know the superlative moment of what it is like to have been "clasped in the arms of Jesus" (Mormon 5:11).

Thomas B. Marsh, once president of the Twelve, was excommunicated, yet he returned. In 1857, he made his way to Salt Lake City, where he spoke in the Bowery and humbly asked for forgiveness. To the congregation he said: "I became jealous of the Prophet, and then I saw double, and overlooked everything that was right, and spent all my time in looking for the evil; . . . I thought I saw a beam in brother Joseph's eye, but it was nothing but a mote, and my own eye was filled with the beam."[9] Those in communities of Saints will love but not follow the disappointed dissenter. Instead, they will help each other to sustain and support the Brethren.

In a community of Saints we not only count our blessings but also weigh them. The special need for a sense of proportion emerges again. Little blessings are still blessings, and they come from the same God as do big blessings. But the big blessings are cause for special rejoicing. It is ironic that often a lack of especially desired little blessings irritates us, even when we are recipients of the supernal blessings given to us by the great atonement, which include the impending glorious resurrection and temple sealings.

Though life in the Church greatly aids our learning, our most vital experiences usually occur in families. There is much to edify in neighborhoods, and in communities, but it is usually in families and small communities where we learn to live right and "to wait." This education of our desires is a vital part of patient enduring. President Joseph F. Smith taught:

> God's ways of educating our desires are, of course, always the most perfect, . . . And what is God's way? Everywhere in nature we are taught the lessons of patience and waiting. We want things a long time before we get them, and the fact that we wanted them a long time makes them all the more precious when they come. In nature we have our seedtime and harvest; and if children were taught that the desires that they sow may be reaped by and by through patience and labor, they will learn to appreciate whenever a long-looked-for goal has been reached. Nature resists us and keeps admonishing us to wait; indeed, we are compelled to wait.[10]

Nevertheless the requirement of enduring causes otherwise good persons to stumble. The Lord still describes as "honorable" those who consistently fall short of being "valiant" in their testimony of Jesus. Truly the gospel net gathers of "every kind" and of every level of commitment (see Matthew 13:47). We can strive for spiritual unity amid such diversity, blending our talents, while moving from honorable to excellent, especially if we help each other.

Yes, the local conditions in which Heavenly Father's children live in their communities of Saints vary widely. But these are all taken into account in His plan of salvation, in which ultimate justice and mercy are assured. When a priesthood leader in India was asked how he handled the pervasive suffering seen in the nation of India, his response was humble and brief: "All people experience some suffering. As for India, we are poor economically, but we are rich in family life. America is rich economically, but increasingly poor in family life!"

Most of all, these communities help us to become and remain "alive in Christ," "one [with] the children of Christ" (2 Nephi 25:25; 4 Nephi 1:17). And being thus enlivened and united, His children will be witnessing children—both to fellow members and to those of the world.

10

WITNESSING FOR THE NAME OF THE LORD JESUS

Willing . . . to stand as witnesses of God at all times and in all things, and in all places . . . even until death (Mosiah 18:9).

One of the most vital things we can do in order to "endure it well" is to believe sufficiently "on the name of the Lord Jesus" that we will "stand as witnesses" for Him in and out of communities of Saints—"at all times and in all things, and in all places" (see D&C 49:12; Mosiah 18:9).

In the biblical sense, a name is intended to convey the *essence* of the individual. "A name is not a mere label of identification; it is an expression of the essential nature of its bearer. A man's name reveals his character."[1]

Consider, therefore, how Jesus Christ always lived up to His names fully. He always carried out the essence of those special names and the roles implicit in those special designations.

In Greek, the name *Jesus* means "God is help" or "Savior."[2] The name *Jesus* was not uncommon. Hence Paul's careful delineation, "Christ Jesus," meaning the Messiah, Jesus (2 Timothy 1:13; 2:1).

The name *Christ* means the "Anointed One," or the "Messiah."[3] *Messiah* denotes "king" or "deliverer." In His mercy the Great Deliverer delivered all mankind from death by His great atonement! Yes, the Jews of that time yearned keenly for deliverance from their political and military bondage, but Jesus, the Messiah, proved to be a far, far greater deliverer.

As to His earlier name, Jehovah, He was and is "the great I Am," and "the Eternal One." Ponder the use of *Jehovah* and *I Am* as testified of in these revelations by the Lord Jehovah:

> His eyes were as a flame of fire; the hair of his head was white like the pure snow; his countenance shone above the brightness of the sun; and his voice was as the sound of the rushing of great waters, even the voice of Jehovah, saying:
> I am the first and the last; I am he who liveth, I am he who was slain; I am your advocate with the Father (D&C 110:3–4).

> Behold, I am he that gave the law, and I am he who covenanted with my people Israel; therefore, the law in me is fulfilled, for I have come to fulfil the law; therefore it hath an end (3 Nephi 15:5).

Thus the essence of Jesus Christ's names tells us much about who He is, what He has done, and what He will yet do. Imbedded in that essence are the implications of His names, too. Therefore, to witness for the name of Jesus Christ is to witness of the reality of His having been anointed as Lord and Savior; to witness of His deeds, especially His atonement; to witness of His attributes; and to witness of the Father's plan of salvation—in which Jesus is the redeeming centerpiece. Jesus' works also witness abundantly for His name. "Have I not delivered you from your enemies, only in that I have left a witness of my name?" (D&C 136:40.) "Jesus answered them, I told you, and ye believed not: the works that I do in my Father's name, they bear witness of me" (John 10:25). "Therefore, hold up your light that it may shine unto the world. Behold I am the light which ye shall hold up—that which ye have seen me do. Behold ye see that I have prayed unto the Father, and ye all have witnessed." (3 Nephi 18:24.)

If the patience or mercy of Jesus were merely like ours, would His arm be "lengthened out all the day long" (2 Nephi 28:32)? And what if His submissiveness were like that of ordinary mortals? In that case, after a few skirmishes with Jewish authorities that demonstrated His obedience to the Father and after having done much good, He could have sought a reasonable settlement instead of marching courageously on to grim Gethsemane and Golgotha.

Apostles are "special witnesses of the name of Christ in all the world" (D&C 107:23). They are to "testify that you have heard my voice, and know my words" (D&C 18:36). However, communities of righteous individuals can witness for Jesus, too. Clearly Church members especially are to be witnesses of Jesus, as is specifically intended in the covenants of the sacramental prayers (see Moroni 4:3; 5:2).

What kind of voice is Jesus'? Most often it is "the voice of the Spirit," which is likened to "the still small voice" (D&C 84:46; 104:36; 85:6). Furthermore, "My voice is Spirit" (D&C 88:66). While literacy in the things of the Spirit is vital, audibility may be no help to the undiscerning—as when "a voice from heaven" was heard, yet some merely "said that it thundered" (John 12:28, 29).

Thus communication from the Lord is most often a voice in which "I will tell you in your mind and in your heart, by the Holy Ghost" (D&C 8:2). Such is "the spirit of revelation" (D&C 8:3). This particular process is the more secure and sure way of revelation.

A comparative few, of course, have had additional and even supernal experiences. President Brigham Young cautioned regarding the durability of flashy and attention-getting forms of witnessing when compared to the witnessing of steady and faithful members who know but do not boast. "Men who have professedly seen the most, known and understood the most, in this Church, and who have testified in the presence of large congregations, in the name of Israel's God, that they have seen Jesus, &c., have been the very men who have left this kingdom, before others who had to live by faith."

> And now Alma began to expound these things unto him, saying: It is given unto many to know the mysteries of God; nevertheless they are laid under a strict command that they shall not impart only according to the portion of his word which he doth grant unto the children of men, according to the heed and diligence which they give unto him (Alma 12:9).

Continuing his counsel, Brigham Young asked: "What made the Twelve Apostles of Jesus Christ witnesses? What constituted them Apostles—special witnesses to the world? Was it seeing miracles? No. What was it? The visions of their minds were opened, and it was necessary that a few should receive light, knowledge, and intelligence, that all the powers of earth and hell could not gainsay or compete with."[4] Minds were opened, since the Lord "will tell you in your mind and in your heart" (D&C 8:2).

Confirming words appear in the Book of Mormon concerning this precious process of coming to know for ourselves: "Behold, I say unto you they are made known unto me by the Holy Spirit of God. Behold, I have fasted and prayed many days that I might know these things of myself. And now I do know of myself that they are true; for the Lord God hath made them manifest unto me by his Holy Spirit; and this is the spirit of revelation which is in me." (Alma 5:46.)

President Marion G. Romney cautioned about the inappropriate sharing of certain spiritual experiences, suggesting that we might have more of them if we would not talk so much about them![5] We must be careful not to "trifle" with sacred things (D&C 6:12).

It was the resurrected Jesus who told the assembled Nephites that they would be "blessed" if they believed in Him *after* they had seen Him. Significantly Jesus then added, *"More blessed* are they who shall believe in your words because that ye shall testify that ye have seen me."* (3 Nephi 12:1–2, emphasis added.)

Orson Pratt said: "If I had seen angels, I might doubt, without having the Holy Ghost. I might doubt if I had seen great miracles, without the Holy Ghost accompanying them; and I might doubt if I saw the heavens opened, if I heard the thunders roll; and I might go and build a golden calf and worship it: but when the Holy Ghost speaks to me and gives me a knowledge that this is the kingdom of God, so that I know it just as well as I know anything else, then that knowledge is past controversy."[6]

President Joseph Fielding Smith taught: "Christ is the second person in the Godhead. But Christ has himself declared that the manifestations we might have of the Spirit of Christ, or from a visitation of an angel, a tangible resurrected being, would not leave the impression and would not convince us and place within us that something which we cannot get away from which we receive through a manifestation of the Holy Ghost. Personal visitations might become dim as time goes on, but this guidance of the Holy ghost is renewed and continued, day after day, year after year, if we live to be worthy of it."[7]

Apostles are also to witness—but so should all true disciples— that salvation and exaltation come *only* through acceptance of the name of the Savior and His ordinances and covenants (see D&C 18:21–28; 107:23, 35). Likewise, only through Christ's atonement are immortality and eternal life made possible through repentance (see D&C 18:11–14). His is the only name under heaven whereby salvation can come (2 Nephi 25:20). Thus we may be "persecuted" and "hated" and slandered for Jesus' name and sake (see Matthew 5:10, 11; 10:22).

Another special way in which we can witness for Jesus is to live as He did. "Now, if ye believe all these things see that ye do them," exhorted King Benjamin (Mosiah 4:10). By the very quality of our lives and by our service to others we are truly witnessing that we do worship Him, that we do remember our covenants with Him, that we do love His gospel, that we do honor the name of Jesus in our daily lives, and that, indeed, we are sufficiently worshipful of Him that we are ever striving to become like Him.

In fact, Christ has directed and invited: "Therefore, what manner of men ought ye to be? Verily I say unto you, even as I am." (3 Nephi 27:27.) Amid the challenges and vicissitudes of life, to be steadily becoming more like Jesus is an especially impressive way to witness for Him.

Having faith on the name of Jesus Christ thus means not only having faith that Jesus is who He declares Himself to be but also knowing and testifying day after day "that he, through his infinite goodness and grace, will keep you through the endurance of faith on his name to the end" (Moroni 8:3).

Ours, therefore, is a continuing task that requires enduring faith in Him and in what His name signifies: "And may the Lord Jesus Christ grant that their prayers may be answered according to their faith; and may God the Father remember the covenant which he hath made with the house of Israel; and may he bless them forever, through faith on the name of Jesus Christ" (Mormon 9:37).

Thus, having real faith in the name of Jesus Christ will ensure that we have "faith unto repentance" (Alma 34:16, 17). Only then will we be fully willing to change and to improve in the very directions prescribed by Jesus, including greater consecration.

No wonder the multiple reinforcing that occurs in the Church is vital! In families, congregations, and Church communities we witness to each other, in word and deed, concerning the name of Jesus. After all, Jesus' atonement with its resultant blessings of a universal resurrection (and eternal life for the most worthy) is the most fundamental act in all human history. What other fact is so deserving of repeated attention in word and deed? Testifying and witnessing for His name, while serving in His name, will help us to qualify for eternal life with Him and with the Father in the ultimate community.

No wonder doing all this is such a fundamental objective. But it also is draining—unless we are renewed! We very much need God's and each other's help in this process. Otherwise we will grow weary and faint in our minds.

11

NOT WEARYING
BY THE WAY

Do not weary by the way, whatever be thy lot
(W. H. Flaville).[1]

If you can force your heart and nerve and sinew
To serve your turn long after they are gone,
And still hold on when there is nothing in you
Except the Will that says to them: Hold on!
(Rudyard Kipling.)[2]

I t is essential to avoid that immobilizing weariness, which can be a prelude to giving up. Professional athletes say that the legs are the first thing to go. In discipleship, the first thing to go is meekness. If a person is not humble, he may, for instance, feel he already knows enough to be bored by any more of the gospel. Hence he need not study. Likewise, if not humble one soon slackens in giving service, ending up merely going through the motions of worship and membership. In such circumstances, lost is the sense of intellectual excitement over the gospel, and also the needed satisfactions and reinforcement that come from serving in the Church.

This boredom and weariness, of course, are self-inflicted. Then, once we are no longer "anxiously engaged," we make ourselves vulnerable to sin (D&C 58:27). Whether through boredom or sin, we slow down or depart from the path. We "faint in [our] minds" and grow stale (Hebrews 12:3). Such intellectual fainting brings a loss of spiritual consciousness, and our strength quickly ebbs.

Physical fatigue, of course, is to be expected. From it we can recover by rest and wise renewal. The form of fatigue noted above, however, can be difficult to recover from unless we can reignite and become, once again, anxiously engaged. So "let us not be weary in well doing: for in due season we shall reap, if we faint not" (Galatians 6:9).

In the particularized renewal of our covenants, in our prayerful pleadings, in and through Church service, and in the renewal of our minds through the study of the "word" and the holy scriptures—in these activities is to be found the fundamental renewal that is vital to the continuing journey of the man and the woman of Christ. For instance, in the renewal of our temple covenants we can be nurtured and encouraged by connecting the present with the past and the future. If we are deprived of these renewing opportunities over a sustained period of time, however, present cares can blur the past and cloud the future.

Special tribute is due, then, to those righteous Church members who do not weary despite sustained adversity, who regularly and quietly endure their special trials in faith day by day. These individuals—and they are all around us—cope with the "short and sharp" trials as well as the "long and tough" ones. The latter involve severe and recurring demands that at times seem even beyond the capacity of these exemplars to meet, yet even in their fatigue and amid the sheer repetitiveness of it all they do not cry out incessantly, "How long, oh Lord, how long!" These who thus inspire the rest of us deserve assurance, and this they should allow to seep into the marrow of their souls. Though still imperfect, they are doing not only the right thing but also the thing that matters most. Moreover, they are doing it far better than they think!

The very nature of the enduring, which is asked of all of us, includes the expenditure of considerable emotional and physical energy, and this over a period of time. Thereby, in this micro-dot called mortality, the faithful experience at least some local taste, as it were, of what lies behind the words concerning God's course being "one eternal round" (D&C 3:2; 35:1).

The very nature of this mortal experience is, as has been said: "The only way to go is through, there isn't any around."

Since discipleship need not be hectic and frantic, we are wise to allow for the periodic compression of experiences and events in our lives. Given the short span of mortality and all that God desires us to do and learn, this should not surprise us. Unless we grasp them firmly and quickly, many of the proffered opportunities to serve have a short shelf life and are perishable. Golden moments come and go. Even full repentance cannot fully recover lost time, though compensatory opportunities will be numerous. President Brigham Young thus urged us to do good whenever we have a chance.[3]

Nevertheless, given the disciple's busy "schedule," helpful counseling and teaching is much needed for the avoidance of weariness: "Teach them to never be weary of good works, but to be meek and lowly in heart; for such shall find rest to their souls" (Alma 37:34). Paradoxical as it sounds, more diligence actually brings more relief. Any selfishness, on the other hand, magnifies our weariness. Selfishness not only shrinks the quantity of service we render but also provides none of the needed renewal, no "rest to [our] souls."

Paul worried, therefore, lest we become impatient and cease "looking unto Jesus" and thereby become "wearied and faint in [our] minds" (Hebrews 12:2–3). If we are not wise, however, both physical and mental fatigue can combine to our great disadvantage, jeopardizing our endurance and limiting our service to others. Jesus saw to this need for His disciples: "And he said unto them, Come ye yourselves apart into a desert place, and rest a while: for there were many coming and going, and they had no leisure so much as to eat. And they departed into a desert place by ship privately." (Mark 6:31–32.)

Thus physical fatigue is surely not all of it. Consider the case of Sidney Rigdon's fainting in his mind. The failure of faith can be a private thing or, as with Sidney Rigdon, a public thing. Of Brother Rigdon's giving up, John Taylor said: "I remember a remark made by Sidney Rigdon—I suppose he did not live his religion—I do not think he did—his knees began to shake in Missouri, and on one occasion he said, 'Brethren, every one of you take your own way, for the work seems as though it [has] come to an end.' Brigham Young encouraged the people, and Joseph Smith told them to be firm and maintain their integrity, for God would be with his people and deliver them."[4]

In the process of enduring, will our knees bend to receive strength or will they shake?

If living our religion can at times make us physically tired, not living it brings a worse weariness, a weariness more pervasive, dark, and constant. The foreseeing Lord in 1831 said of Sidney Rigdon that he had "exalted himself in his heart, and received not counsel, but grieved the Spirit" (D&C 63:55). Sidney Rigdon's ego apparently was not fully tamed. The Lord counseled him, "remain with my people," but he did not (D&C 124:104).

Looking unto Jesus involves not only taking His yoke upon us but also keeping it there: "Take my yoke upon you, and learn of me; for I am meek and lowly in heart: and ye shall find rest unto your souls" (Matthew 11:29). Enduring is easier when accompanied by our meekness and lowliness. One of the most relieving experiences, which is designed to keep us from fainting, occurs when the Lord speaks "peace to [our minds]" (D&C 6:23).

The Lord warned, "All those who will not endure chastening, but deny me, cannot be sanctified" (D&C 101:5). This linking of failure to endure with denying the Lord suggests a failure of trust in the purposes and designs of Heavenly Father's plan. Laman and Lemuel grew weary, murmured, and even rebelled, because they "knew not the dealings" of God (1 Nephi 2:12). Others of us may likewise crack under the refining heat of a particular trial because we doubt or deny "the design . . . and the glory which shall follow after much tribulation" (D&C 58:3).

It is not real faith, therefore, to say, in effect, "Yes, there is a God, but He is not to be trusted when it comes to our personal trials." On the other hand, trusting in the Refiner's love, purposes, and timing reflects a multi-faceted faith.

Willing engagement hastens consecration and carries with it promises both crucial and specific: "And any man that shall go and preach this gospel of the kingdom, and fail not to continue faithful in all things, *shall not be weary in mind*, neither darkened, neither in body, limb, nor joint; and a hair of his head shall not fall to the ground unnoticed. And they shall not go hungry, neither athirst." (D&C 84:80; emphasis added.)

If faithful, we will thereby experience this "renewing of [our] bodies" (D&C 84:33). If we are not specifically focused, however, we will tire in both body and mind—a dual drain. As the Brethren of today gladly attest, amid aging and jet lagging, the Lord keeps His promise of renewal.

One major cause of real fatigue, little appreciated by those so afflicted, is trying to serve two masters. This is devastating double duty. If so divided, one inevitably ends up being ineffective, even

disloyal, in respect to one master or another—a most fatiguing cir-
cumstance. (Matthew 6:24.)

Insincerity is fatiguing, too. Anne Morrow Lindbergh wrote of
the need "to shed my Martha-like anxiety about many things. . . .
shedding pride. . . . shedding hypocrisy in human relationships.
What a rest that will be! The most exhausting thing in life, I have
discovered, is being insincere. That is why so much of social life is
exhausting."[5]

Brigham Young counseled us to control our tempers, even
when we are provoked, because this helps us to avoid another
form of exhaustion: the auger that anger can become. "Never suffer anger to find a seat in your breast, never get angry. Treat all
mildly, govern yourselves, control your passions, and it will give
you power."[6] In the same way that aggressive, evil thoughts
should not be offered a chair and invited to sit down, so anger
should never be an overnight guest!

> If we will school ourselves and bring our own tempers and disposi-
> tions into subjection we shall then have influence to do good, over
> the minds of our acquaintances; but if we do not control ourselves
> how can we have influence over others?[7]

> If you give way to your angry feelings, it sets on fire the whole
> course of nature, and is set on fire of hell; and you are then apt to set
> those on fire who are contending with you. When you feel as though
> you would burst, tell the old boiler to burst, and just laugh at the
> temptation to speak evil. If you will continue to do that, you will
> soon be so masters of yourselves as to be able, if not to tame, to con-
> trol your tongues,—able to speak when you ought, and to be silent
> when you ought.[8]

Hence, self-control avoids many otherwise wearying conflagrations.

This self-control can spare us another portion of weariness,
one that results from the management of conflict in our human
relationships—few things than which are more draining and worrying. Thus we need not experience all of the grinding weariness
that comes of conflict. Calmness conserves energy as well as relationships.

We will not, of course, be able to manage all the outcomes of
all the conflicts and certainly not the behavior of others involved.
But we can manage ourselves in the midst of those conflicts and

better influence others. When, through meekness and lowliness, we control our egos, we will not experience the extra weariness that is demanded by the exercise of unrighteous dominion. That dominion involves its own form of added calisthenics, not the least of which is resisting one's conscience. By contrast, enduring well brings a joy that displaces despair.

Yet without the tension of decision-making amid opposites and among shades of gray that is more easily managed by righteous reflexes, life really would be an undifferentiated "compound in one" (2 Nephi 2:11). Without moral agency the taste buds of the soul could not function fully. Without an "opposition in all things" there could not be the isometrics required for individual development as the old self is pitted against the new. Hence, neither happiness nor misery (see v. 23). God has yet to tell us all the implications of having things in a "compound of one," but we can be certain they have to do with what is needed in order that we "might have joy" (2 Nephi 2:25).

If we are focused on Jesus and His work, both our joys and our staying capacity are increased: "Blessed art thou, Nephi, for those things which thou hast done; for I have beheld how thou hast with unwearyingness declared the word, which I have given unto thee, unto this people. And thou hast not feared them, and hast not sought thine own life, but hast sought my will, and to keep my commandments." (Helaman 10:4.) Nephi had not selfishly sought his "own life," but rather had sought to do God's will. This gave him the extra and undivided energy which made his striving with unwearied diligence possible. Nephi knew in which direction he faced: toward God.

In contrast, and to be pitied, are the ambivalent, forever pivoting as between looking toward God or man. With all the incessant pivoting, no wonder some grow so weary! Instead, if we let our own wills be swallowed up in the will of the Lord, there is a more holistic deployment of our talents (see Mosiah 15:7). Like Nephi, we are not to pursue our own wills.

Another vital source of renewal is expending some of our energy by striving with the less active. Serving in this way keeps the giver from becoming weary or from fainting in his mind, making possible "striving with unwearied diligence that they may bring the remainder of their brethren to the knowledge of the truth; therefore there are many who do add to their numbers daily"

(Helaman 15:6). Assisting in such reclamation actually gives us added energy. We are energized and empowered, like the father of the prodigal, who ran to greet him "when he was yet a great way off" (Luke 15:20). Such real love keeps us from becoming too tired to reach out.

We can, in fact, become "alive in Christ because of our faith" (2 Nephi 25:25). No wonder those who respond to the invitation to "come unto Christ" (D&C 20:59) "talk of Christ . . . rejoice in Christ . . . [and] preach of Christ . . . that [their] children may know to what source they may look" (2 Nephi 25:28). They know the Lord will "comfort [their] soul in Christ" and help them to "endure it well" (Alma 31:31–32). It is fitting that when those who were once lost manage to come home they are rightfully and enthusiastically described as being "alive again" (Luke 15:32).

When so engaged in these various forms of service, will we still have cares? Oh, yes! However, we have the invitation "cast all your care upon Him" (1 Peter 5:7). Only He can carry all our cares, anyway. No wonder we are to talk, preach, and rejoice in Christ, ever knowing to whom to look (2 Nephi 25:26).

Weariness also arises out of struggling to perform in a lackluster way because of a lack of commitment. Trying to do the Lord's work with a slothful heart brings its own special buildup of blockage in arteries and valves. There are no aerobics in apathy. Merely going through the motions of Church membership without the renewing emotions of discipleship can be very fatiguing.

Where there is any such slackness, the divine word about avoiding fainting in our minds and promising the renewing of our bodies cannot be fully obtained. Nor can we receive the special peace and rest that Jesus promises. "Peace I leave with you, my peace I give unto you: not as the world giveth, give I unto you. Let not your heart be troubled, neither let it be afraid." (John 14:27; see also Matthew 11:28.)

If, along with other things, we will be meek, search the scriptures, proclaim the gospel, and seek to reclaim our less-active brothers and sisters, we will avoid the needless weariness of mind and body that would otherwise beset us. After all, it was in the midst of his heavy work of reactivation, bringing souls again unto Christ, that Nephi received this counsel: "Yea, I say unto you, that the more part of [the Lamanites] are doing this, and they are striving with unwearied diligence that they may bring the remainder of their brethren to the knowledge of the truth; therefore there are many who do add to their numbers daily" (Helaman 15:6).

Jesus, who bore the greatest and heaviest burdens, knows how to help His followers absorb afflictions in a unique way: "And the Lord provided for them that they should hunger not, neither should they thirst; yea, and he also gave them strength, that they should suffer no manner of afflictions, save it were swallowed up in the joy of Christ. Now this was according to the prayer of Alma; and this because he prayed in faith." (Alma 31:38.)

Even so, we will not be free of affliction. But we will be given help in bearing affliction, especially if our wills are swallowed up in the will of the Father and Christ. Being swallowed up in the will of God can help us cope not only with afflictions but even with death (see Mosiah 16:8; Alma 22:14).

It is noteworthy that this particular prophet, Alma, while trying to reactivate people, was efficient, because he was determined to "try the virtue of the word of God," the very approach which has "a great tendency to lead the people to do that which [is] just" (Alma 31:5).

Having faith in Jesus includes having faith in the assurance that our trials and difficulties "are but for a small moment," even when at the moment they seem to us to be extended and unremitting (D&C 122:4). Faith includes having faith in God's timing.

As we see the valiant reach breaking points without breaking, it inspires the rest of us to trust in the divine design in our own circumstances, which may not be immediately apparent to us during our trials: "Ye cannot behold with your natural eyes, for the present time, the design of your God . . . and the glory which shall follow after much tribulation" (D&C 58:3). Furthermore, the empathy earned by our patiently enduring will be eternal and will bless others in the world to come, just as it blesses some in special ways now. A special and helpful form of multilinguality emerges too. Annie Sophie Swetchine said: "Those who have suffered much are like those who know many languages: they have learned to understand and be understood by all."[9] By His unique obedience and suffering Jesus was made unique and perfect in His understanding.

Everlastingly relevant is submissiveness to God, the admission ticket to blessings of unspeakable proportions that await and that are part of the promised divine and everlasting rest. It was not only the Prophet Joseph Smith but also all the faithful who were told, "if thou endure it well" (D&C 121:8), "all these things shall give thee experience and shall be for thy good" (D&C 122:7).

We may murmur a little now over the calisthenics of being stretched, and we may complain over enduring the exhausting isometrics of individual development in the mortal gymnasium. But if we were deprived of all these experiences in mortality, how would we feel later, as immortals, upon discovering that our smallness of stature was due to that earlier deprivation?

Of course there are strains and stresses. We have even been assured that some of the needed purifications and siftings are accomplished by such trials (see D&C 100:16; 136:31). Indeed, the increasing polarities in the world between righteousness and wickedness will hasten such siftings. If we wish to help those weak in the faith who may falter, we will strengthen our own faith and then endure for their sakes as well. It is difficult, as Jesus implied to Peter, to strengthen our brethren unless we ourselves are converted (see Luke 22:32). And the more "settled" we are in our minds and hearts, the more we can help others.

We can "bear one another's burdens, that they may be light" not only by rendering whatever practical assistance is needed, along with the empathy and the sympathy, but also by bearing up under our own burdens. Courage can be contagious. It is similar with comforting "those that stand in need of comfort," by means of which we stand "as witnesses of God at all times and in all things, and in all places" (Mosiah 18:8–9).

Finally, it is worth remembering that there is often a resistant residue of feeling, concerning which President Ezra Taft Benson counseled: "There are times when you simply have to righteously hang on and outlast the devil until his depressive spirit leaves you."[10]

While carrying our individual crosses, we can greatly help each other if we "hold fast" to the doctrines as well as to each other.

12

ENDURING
IT WELL

No matter how serious the trial, how deep the distress, how great the affliction, [God] will never desert us. He never has, and He never will. He cannot do it. It is not His character. He is an unchangeable being; the same yesterday, the same today, and He will be the same throughout the eternal ages to come. We have found that God. We have made Him our friend, by obeying His Gospel; and He will stand by us. We may pass through the fiery furnace; we may pass through deep waters; but we shall not be consumed nor overwhelmed. We shall emerge from all these trials and difficulties the better and purer for them, if we only trust in our God and keep His commandments. (George Q. Cannon.)[1]

I will not, I cannot, desert to his foes ("How Firm a Foundation").[2]

To think of enduring to the end as "hanging in there" and "holding fast" is certainly not inaccurate. But even swaying seaweed knows how to "hold fast." Enduring to the end, then, is more than weaving and surviving. Instead, we are called upon to "endure in faith" and "endure it well" and endure "valiantly" (see D&C 101:35; D&C 121:8, 29). Nephi's imagery conveys a special zestfulness: "Wherefore, ye must press forward with a steadfastness in Christ, having a perfect brightness of hope, and a love of God and of all men. Wherefore, if ye shall press forward, feasting upon the word of Christ, and endure to the end, behold, thus saith the Father: Ye shall have eternal life." (2 Nephi 31:20.)

Here Nephi portrays an earnest enthusiasm, but without illusions. Hence *dullness* is not descriptive of such disciples. *Bored* is the wrong word to describe such believers. *Casual* is not the correct connotation for such committed climbers on the straight and narrow path. This journey will finally require all we have, yet at the end of the journey, after we "endure it well," we will receive "all" that God has (D&C 84:38). There isn't any more than that!

Enduring, then, is much more than making a passive passage. Rather it is an activism that not only affirms one's faith but also confirms the basic joys of life. Until the end, enduring is not over. In fact it may be more of a challenge as life goes on. For some, life's final exams may turn out to be more difficult than the midterms, and certainly than the early quizzes. Hence the high relevance of the prepositional phrase "to the end."

Given the uneven seasons of life, the Lord desires balance in His disciples as well as in the Church collectively. We cannot be all sail and no anchor. Moreover, as we grow, "the root and the top" should be "equal in strength," providing a capacity to endure both heat and storm (Jacob 5:66).

Hence we are not merely to exist to the end but are to persist in coping with what is occurring in the holy present. If we will follow the example of "the Son of the living God," great things await us (see 2 Nephi 31:16). "Nevertheless, he that endureth in faith and doeth my will, the same shall overcome, and shall receive an inheritance upon the earth when the day of transfiguration shall come" (D&C 63:20). "And all they who suffer persecution for my name, and endure in faith, though they are called to lay down their lives for my sake yet shall they partake of all this glory" (D&C 101:35).

Even yesterday's spiritual experience, however, does not guarantee us against tomorrow's relapse. Persistence thus matters greatly. More than a few, for instance, have had supernal, spiritual experiences only to fall away later; or, more often, merely to pull off to the side of the road, though intending only a brief rest stop.

Hence the emphasis on enduring well to the end is wise, simply because we are at risk till the end! By enduring well all along the way we can, for example, have felicity amid poverty and gratitude without plentitude. We can even have meekness amid injustice. One never sees the "root of bitterness springing up" in enduring disciples (Hebrews 12:15). If we are wise like Job, while in the midst of "all these things," including the customized chastening, we too will avoid charging God foolishly (see Job 1:22).

Included in the enduring process is meeting the test of being constantly improved. Remodeling is costly and painful. But how can we realistically expect the arduous process of putting off the old man and putting on the new man to be otherwise?

God has repeatedly said He would structure mortality to be a proving and testing experience (see Abraham 3:25; Mosiah 23:21). Hence our fiery trials, said Peter, should not be thought of as "some strange thing" (1 Peter 4:12). Still some of us approach our experience in this mortal school as if it were to be mostly relaxing recesses with only the occasional irritant of summoning bells. In fact, any recesses are merely for renewal and for catching one's breath; and these are not to become a prolonged sigh of relief that introduces protracted leisure or languor.

By taking Jesus' yoke upon us we learn most deeply of Him, and especially how to be like Him. This includes emulating His power to endure (see Matthew 11:29). Even though our experiences are micro compared to His, the process is the same. True enduring, therefore, represents not merely the passage of time but also the passage of the soul—not merely going from A to B, but the "mighty change"—all the way from A to Z.

Rather than resigned shoulder-shrugging, enduring involves soul trembling. After all, Jesus bled not at a few pores but "at every pore" (D&C 19:18). He, the Lord of the universe, actually trembled because of pain!

The enveloping dissonance that sometimes accompanies our enduring can bring discovery—new ways of knowing about ourselves and about our larger-than-imagined reserves. These discoveries might not occur without shaking up the status quo. But we do not like it—"no chastening for the present seemeth to be joyous" (Hebrews 12:11). As to testing faith, C.S. Lewis said: "You never know how much you really believe anything until its truth or falsehood becomes a matter of life and death to you. It is easy to say you believe a rope to be strong and sound as long as you are merely using it to cord a box. But suppose you had to hang by that rope over a precipice. Wouldn't you then first discover how much you really trusted it?"

Speaking of the pain that accompanies suffering, Lewis also perceptively observed: "It doesn't really matter whether you grip the arms of the dentist's chair or let your hands lie in your lap. The drill drills on."[3]

This dual need for testing and discovering is the reason why some of our trials and experiences in life cannot be cut short. Therefore, more than curtain parting is needed. We must enter into what is discovered. One does not graduate in mid-academic year, anyway. So the risks for us are real, and they persist to the end. This is one reason why the unconverted and unrooted are usually the first to let go, enduring "but for a time" (Mark 4:17). "The seed that falls by the way side, for want of root cannot endure the scorching sun of persecution. Those who are represented by the seed among thorns cannot endure because of the cares of the world and the pride of life. The influence and power of the world, and of the adversary, surrounding such individuals, they are by and by turned away, and cease to be Saints, cease to serve the Lord, and turn every one to his own way."[4]

The assurance that the Lord's grace is sufficient for the meek does not mean an absence of adversity or a promise of repose and ease. His grace, instead, does bring the needed inner strength and peace that are vital in the process of enduring all things (see Ether 12:26).

Brigham wisely counseled, "We must endure all things that we cannot help."[5] How many times we fret and stew over what we cannot change! This is understandable but regrettable. "The Almighty has his objects and plans all laid, and we are to pass through all these afflictions and to endure all that he calls us to endure, to give us knowledge, wisdom, and experience; for we cannot receive them upon any other principle."[6]

Even when we may be enduring reasonably well in other respects, we are not enduring well if we murmur. Murmuring is defined as a half-suppressed resentment or muttered complaint. Just as "a yawn [can be] a silent shout," so murmuring can be much more than muted muttering. Realized or not, the real "addressee" of some of our murmuring is clearly the Lord, as when the people complained against Moses (see Exodus 16:8; 1 Nephi 16:20).

Murmuring, however, comes naturally to the natural man. It crosses the scriptural spectrum of recorded complaints. Grecian widows were felt to be neglected in favor of the Hebrews (Acts 6:1). We need bread. We need water (see Numbers 21:5). "Why did we ever leave Egypt?" (See Numbers 11:20.) "Why did we ever leave Jerusalem?" (See 1 Nephi 2:11.) Some murmured over persecution by unbelievers, while others even murmured over what the name of Christ's Church should be (see Mosiah 27:1; 3 Nephi 27:3–4).

The real danger, of course, is that we will finally start believing in our own murmuring! Too much such catharsis, and we really think we are experiencing too many "raw deals." Good-bye then to operative faith in Heavenly Father's plan of salvation. How can the whole plan be "OK" if our portion of it seems so awry?

A basic cause of murmuring is that too many of us seem to expect that life will flow ever smoothly, featuring, as it were, an unbroken chain of green lights with empty parking places just in front of our destinations. It is often the little things that get to us. Benjamin Disraeli, who had many large pressures as prime minister, confessed, "I can bear a great reverse, but these petty personal vexations throw one off one's balance."[7]

There was murmuring, too, because Nephi broke his steel bow and also because he couldn't possibly build a ship (see 1 Nephi 16:18–20; 17:17). Those same murmurers, insensitive to their inconsistency, quickly surfeited themselves on the meat brought back by Nephi's new bow. They also sailed successfully over vast oceans to a new hemisphere in the ship that Nephi couldn't build. Strange, isn't it, how those with the longest lists of new demands also have the shortest memories of past blessings?

How handy, too, imperfect leaders always are as focal points for the frustrations of some, especially if particular circumstances require the leaders for good reason to suffer in silence! But having confidence in leaders who keep confidences is part of sustaining them.

In the late 1820s Brigham Young, as yet untouched by the restored gospel, was a somewhat discouraged young man. Apparently he found himself disapproving of much of what he saw in the world, while wondering if he had a work yet to do. His loving brother Phineas gave Brigham prescient counsel: "Hang on, for I know the Lord is agoing to do some thing for us."[8] What soon happened to Brigham and because of him is Moses-like history!

We must never underestimate the difficulty of the last days, however. Joel and Zephaniah both speak of the last times as being "a day of gloominess" (Joel 2:2; Zephaniah 1:15). The coming decades will be decades of despair. Why? Especially because, as Moroni said, despair comes of iniquity (see Moroni 10:22). The more iniquity, the more despair. Therefore, unless there is widespread repentance, despair will both deepen and spread—except among those who have gospel gladness.

As with Paul, however, though we may be momentarily perplexed, we need not despair: "We are troubled on every side, yet not distressed; we are perplexed, but not in despair" (2 Corinthians 4:8). Likewise, if we are prepared spiritually, we need not fear (see D&C 38:30). Puzzlement, for instance, is often the knob on the door of insight. The knob must be grasped with firm faith and deliberately turned in order for one to see and to experience what lies beyond.

Upon arriving at the foreseen geographical destination, President Brigham Young confirmed, "This is the place!" Of God's plan of salvation with its developmental destination, it can be confirmed, "This is the process!"

In the midst of our afflictions, reassurances will come to us from the Lord and from His prophets. The Lord's people in another age feared an approaching army, and their prophet reassured them; and "therefore they hushed their fears" (Mosiah 23:28). Prophets in our time will occasionally need to hush our fears, too.

The Lord has clearly indicated that His purifying and sifting judgment will begin "at the house of God" (see 1 Peter 4:17; D&C 112:25). Just what this sifting will consist of is not now clear. In a worsening world, special pressures will combine with the ongoing and demanding daily rigors of "taking up the cross daily" (see Luke 9:23). The tempter's triad of tools are temptation, persecution, and tribulation (see Matthew 13:18–22). These tools will be relentlessly used upon God's flock (see Matthew 13:21; Luke 8:13). And if the heat from the summer sun of such circumstances will scorch even a green tree, that heat upon the whole world will be intense (see Luke 23:31; D&C 135:6; Alma 32:38).

The cares and anxieties of the world are pervasive and persistent. They also vary widely from person to person. But it is usually the case (whatever the objective load of these cares is and even if it is actually small) that these worries will expand so as to fill whatever worry space is available in that individual. Thus what may be an easily manageable load for one person may seem overwhelming to another. Hence the need for us to put in perspective the cares and anxieties of the world. Otherwise the cares and anxieties will spread, crowding out space needed for spiritual things.

Though we may still let things "get to us" at times, there is no need for us to be threatened in any fundamental ways. There is no need for trembling, for instance, over the prospects of the annihilation of our species. Similarly we have no need to fret over the lack of meaning in life, or of identity, or of the existence of a loving God.

It is well, then, to put the cares of the day and the anxieties of the moment in the context of the things of eternity. After all, the little things are little.

Peter and Paul urged us to become "grounded," "rooted," "established," and "settled" (Colossians 1:23; 2:7; Ephesians 3:17). Being thus settled does not immunize us against trials, but it does against concerns over the basic realities about God, life, meaning, and the universe. We can and will be tried tactically, but this can occur without our calling into question the whole strategy of God's plan of salvation. Enduring involves coping with those moments when we cannot give an easy explanation for what is happening to us or around us, but we can still know that God loves us (see 1 Nephi 11:17).

Once again, let us not forget the simple little modifying phrase, "to the end." Once again, too, going 60 percent of the way will not do.

Some reasons why it is so hard to endure have been explored in previous pages. Sometimes we just plain feel put upon. We are doing the large things pretty well, so why must we put up with the "petty vexations" and frustrations? A reasonable answer is that our personal development requires us to pass through the little things too in order to give us full perspective and broad patience. If we enjoyed immunity from all the little things, would we later belong in the same company with those who endured both the little and the large challenges and who overcame them?

After the Atonement and its related agonies, Jesus does not mention such matters as how keenly He thirsted, or the sting of the scourging. But these and other comparatively "little" things He experienced were certainly trying and real, and He endured them even as He simultaneously worked out the large and great deliverance for all mankind that would bless billions and billions.

Nephi's broken bow doubtless brought to him some irritation, but not immobilizing bitterness. After all, he was just trying to feed the extended family, so why should he have to contend as well with a broken bow? Yet out of that episode came a great teaching moment. Irritation often precedes instruction. If we are not careful, small things can become the small sifting holes through which our resolve trickles away.

The thought evokes a further question: In the process of developing the precious quality of empathy, would we trade for some earlier relief today the enlarged empathy to be used in so many endless tomorrows? Would we trade keener perceptivity, likewise to be used throughout time and eternity, for an abrupt, premature closing up of today's upsetting scene? Without eternal perspectives, we might.

God our Eternal Father is very serious about developing in us the eternal attributes. It is well that we focus more on our eternal possibilities, because, as Brigham Young put it, "man possesses the germ of all the attributes and power that are possessed by God . . . that God possesses in perfection." Moreover, with almost stunning insight he counseled, "sin is . . . an inversion of the attributes God has placed in [man]."[9] These words suggest, for example, that the innate and needed desire we have to succeed, when gone awry, leads to putting others down. Furthermore, the quality of patience, if skewed, could lead to a squandering indulgence, and the virtue of meekness could be distorted to mean sublimation to various peer groups or Caesars, or a refusal to choose independently for ourselves. The quality of submissiveness could be distorted into a feeling of diffused accountability and responsibility for ourselves. The innate sense of identity can quickly sour into pride. Likewise, love can be twisted into lust and perversion. Thus, as immortal genes are mixed in with the natural man's challenges of the flesh, "inversion" can occur—unless there is a conversion to the ways of the Lord.

No wonder, therefore, in our development that some events almost seem to wait upon the successful completion of an eternal spiritual transaction. Then the things of the day become almost inconsequential.

Sometimes our pleadings are for relief, but not for ourselves; rather, for a loved one. These can be noble requests. But if these importunings go unanswered, can we endure well? This denial may be for the same, sober reasons why our importunings for ourselves cannot always be granted to us. Therefore, will we also have faith in Heavenly Father's "designs" for our loved ones? (See D&C 58:3, 4.)

Even when special nobility underlies one's petition to God, then, this cannot always be the controlling factor. Nor can one's personal deservingness. Consider Jesus in Gethsemane!

Small wonder, given such tutorial purposes, that both President John Taylor and President Brigham Young later testified that they were glad their earlier views about the need for relieving certain human suffering had not prevailed.[10]

We may wonder how our joy can be full in eternity if anyone we love is excluded from a fulness of joy? Can Adam and Eve have complete joy without having their unrighteous posterity with them, including Cain, in the eternal world to come (see D&C 107:53–56)?

On a much more vast scale, can Heavenly Father and Mother have a fullness of joy when a third of their children rebelled early on—along with many more later who will never come finally and fully home?

Mitigating factors to be considered include these: (1) In the justice and mercy of God, everyone will—at one point or another—have had an adequate opportunity to choose their futures according to the acted out "desires of their hearts." (2) Having chosen for ourselves that which we will be allotted in eternity, we will not later complain about God's mercy or justice (see Mosiah 27:31; Alma 12:15; Mosiah 6:1). Brigham affirms: "If we fail to obtain the salvation we are seeking for, we shall acknowledge that we have secured to ourselves every reward that is due to us by our acts, and that we have acted in accordance with the independent agency given us, and we shall be judged out of our own mouths whether we are justified or condemned."[11] (3) Each post-resurrection kingdom is a kingdom of glory that is far better than this world we now know. Even "the glory of the telestial" will surpass "all understanding" (D&C 76:89). (4) The family circle, when finally completed in time for the world to come, may yet be larger than we may now imagine; late arrivals, after having paid a severe price and thus being finally qualified, may be more than a few.

We must not, therefore, underestimate the redemptive and reaching effectiveness of our Father's ongoing work in the spirit world. Even so, being a "trembling parent" here should cause us to be more conscientious now while there is yet time to affect eternity (see 2 Nephi 1:14).

After all, the resurrected Jesus, while visiting the Nephites and after blessing the children, said, "Now behold, my joy is full!" (3 Nephi 17:20.) Yet He clearly knew that many elsewhere on the planet were lost and beyond conversion. Earlier, and a continent away, He had rejoiced in prayer over the original Twelve, noting, however, that He had lost one, Judas (John 17:12). Therefore, it is apparently possible to have a fullness of joy even when some have been lost.

In any case we will not be frozen forever in grief over what might have been. This will be especially so when we "see things as they really are" and "things as they really will be"—for all of these will demonstrate God's surpassing mercy and astounding generosity (Jacob 4:13). Those who receive lesser kingdoms, but still kingdoms of glory, will not question; nor, therefore, should we question in anticipatory ways. The justice and mercy of God, who is perfect in His love, will prevail. He who is perfect in determining individual accountability is likewise perfect in His generosity and mercy in His bestowals upon His children.

Nevertheless, ever to be born in mind is a preexisting, flinty fact: God, Himself, either cannot change or, in His infinite love and wisdom, will not change the reality that the moral agency of every individual cannot be violated!

Yes, having to choose is an onerous burden at times, but the prophetic and strategic words are: "Therefore, cheer up your hearts, and remember that ye are free to act for yourselves—to choose the way of everlasting death or the way of eternal life" (2 Nephi 10:23). This cosmic fact becomes the great hinge upon which swing all the different outcomes in terms of salvation and exaltation.

Meanwhile, God "allotteth unto men" certain things, and with these we are to be content (see Alma 29:4; Philippians 4:11; 1 Timothy 6:8). A missing parent or limb is to be lived without. Other things are to be endured and "lived with."

Temper and lust are to be tamed and expunged (see 3 Nephi 12:22, 28). One's race is fixed, yet he or she may be among those granted by the Lord in that "nation and tongue, to teach his word" (Alma 29:8). One's genetic endowment is fixed but carries with it a duty to be a careful steward thereof.

The submissive soul will thus be led aright. Though living within certain limitations—enduring some things well, and being "anxiously engaged" in setting other things right—the disciple all the while discerns the difference between what is allotted and what is required (see Alma 29:3, 6, 7).

Within what is allotted to us, we can "endure it well," such as taking one more step when we think we cannot, making it to the next ridge when we are sure it is too far. Likewise, enduring injustice, misrepresentation, irony, and abuse, because we are the servants of Him upon whom wicked men spat.

Yes, at times during the journey of discipleship we will be frustrated by lesser things. The irritations and diversions do seem to "get in the way." We would do well, however, to contemplate some details along Jesus' road through Gethsemane and on to Calvary and all He encountered amid His accomplishment of the astonishing atonement. Did there need to be the added frustration of having to attend to Peter's impulsive severing of an assailant's ear? Was it really necessary to have a thief on an adjoining cross, pleading his personal case just when Jesus was saving all mankind? Was it really necessary, too, for Jesus to endure thirst while hanging on the cross? Many little things were part of that big moment!

Yet without all those little things, could it later have been correctly declared, "He that ascended up on high . . . also . . . descended below all things, in that he comprehend all things"? (D&C 88:6.)

Ever ringing in our ears, therefore, whenever we are asked to "endure it well," should be the Savior's searching question in Doctrine and Covenants 122:8: "The Son of Man hath descended below them all. Art thou greater than he?"

EPILOGUE

SUBMISSION
By Neal A. Maxwell

When from Thy stern tutoring
I would quickly flee,
Turn me from my Tarshish
To where is best for me.

Help me in my Nineveh
To serve with love and truth—
Not on a hillside posted
Mid shade of gourd or booth.

When my modest suffering seems
So vexing, wrong, and sore,
May I recall what freely flowed
From each and every pore.

Dear Lord of the Abba Cry,
Help me in my duress
To endure it well enough
And to say, . . . "Nevertheless."

NOTES

Chapter 1
Enduring to the End

1. William Makepeace Thackeray, in John Bartlett, *Familiar Quotations* (Boston: Little, Brown and Company, 1980), p. 540.
2. Brigham Young, in *Journal of Discourses* 1:338 (hereafter cited as *JD*).
3. Thomas H. Johnson, ed., *The Complete Poems of Emily Dickinson* (Boston: Little, Brown and Company, 1960), p. 148.
4. Forrest Morgan, ed., *The Works of Walter Bagehot* (Hartford: The Travelers Insurance Company, 1889), p. 313.
5. Robert Rhodes James, ed., *Churchill Speaks* (New York: Chelsea House, 1980), p. 771.
6. Will Durant, *The Story of Philosophy* (New York: Garden City Publishing Company, 1927), p. 1.
7. In Thomas F. Hornbein, *Everest—The West Ridge,* ed. David Brower (San Francisco: Sierra Club, 1965), p. 100.

Chapter 2
Following Fixed Principles amid Commotion

1. Brigham Young, in *JD* 13:280.
2. William Manchester, *A World Lit Only by Fire* (Boston: Little, Brown and Company, 1992), pp. 26–27.
3. Jose Ortega y Gasset, *The Modern Theme,* James Cleugh, trans. (New York: Harper & Brothers, 1961), p. 29.
4. Ed. Rubenstein, "The Economics of Crime," *Imprimis,* August 1995, p. 3.
5. "We Thank Thee, O God, for a Prophet," *Hymns,* 1985, no. 19.

Chapter 3
Pressing Forward in the Days Ahead

1. Winston Churchill, in address at Harrow School on 29 October 1941, quoted in *Churchill Speaks,* p. 772.
2. *Vital Speeches of the Day,* 15 October 1995, p. 17.
3. *Vital Speeches,* p. 18.
4. Patrick F. Fagan, *Imprimis,* October 1995, p. 4.
5. Gertrude Himmelfarb, *The De-Moralization of Society* (New York: Alfred A. Knopf, 1995), p. 253.
6. "The Talk of the Town," *The New Yorker,* 30 August 1976, p. 22.
7. Matthew Robinson, *Investor's Business Daily,* 16 October 1995.
8. G. K. Chesterton, *The Everlasting Man* (Garden City, New York: Image Books, 1955), p. 148.
9. David Popenoe, "American Family Decline, 1960–1990: A Review and Appraisal," *Journal of Marriage and the Family,* August 1993, p. 540.
10. In *Generation at the Crossroads* (New Brunswick, New Jersey: Rutgers University Press, 1994), p. 126.
11. See Neil Postman, Technopoly (New York: Alfred A. Knopf, 1992), p. 75.
12. "Choruses from 'the Rock,'" in *T.S. Eliot, The Complete Poems and Plays 1909–1950* (New York: Harcourt, Brace & World, Inc., 1952), p. 96.
13. Conference Report, April 1958, pp. 96–97.
14. Cited in Richard Betts, "Analysis, War, and Decision: Why Intelligence Failures Are Inevitable," *World Politics,* October 1978, p. 62.
15. See *TPJS,* p. 220. See also D&C 130:7; 1 Nephi 9:6.
16. In *JD* 12:256.

Chapter 4
Pursuing Discipleship in a Living Church

1. Brigham Young in *JD* 18:246–47.
2. *JD* 5:75.
3. *JD* 10:221, emphasis added.
4. Brigham Young, in *JD* 7:133–34.
5. Stuart W. Smith, ed., *Douglas Southall Freeman on Leadership* (Newport, Rhode Island: Naval War College Press, 1990), pp. 35, 40, 42.
6. David O. McKay, in Conference Report, April 1964, p. 5.

7. Anthony Kenny, *Thomas More* (New York: Oxford University Press, 1983), p. 88.

8. *JD* 14:97.

9. *JD* 11:257.

10. *JD* 1:358–59. See also 2 Nephi 2:11.

11. *History of the Church* 4:164.

Chapter 5
Pursuing Consecration

1. Brigham Young, in *JD* 9:149. See also John 7:17.

2. Brigham Young, in *JD* 12:99, emphasis added.

3. *Lectures on Faith* 3:2–5.

4. See Andrew F. Ehat and Lyndon W. Cook, eds., *The Words of Joseph Smith* (Provo: BYU Religious Studies Center, 1980), pp. 41, 50, 51.

5. C.S. Lewis, *Mere Christianity* (New York: The Macmillan Company, 1960), p. 160.

6. "We Are All Enlisted," *Hymns*, 1985, no. 250.

7. Joseph F. Smith, *Gospel Doctrine* (Salt Lake City: Deseret Book Company, 1939), p. 297.

8. In *JD* 14:361.

9. In *JD* 18:247.

10. "More Holiness Give Me," *Hymns*, 1985, no. 131.

11. See *JD* 14:360.

12. In *JD* 5:352.

13. See *TPJS*, p. 220.

14. "Law and Manners," *Atlantic Monthly*, July 1924, p. 1.

Chapter 6
Living amid So Great a Cloud of Witnesses

1. Brigham Young once defined faith as faith in Jesus' name, in His character, in His atonement, and in the Father's plan of salvation (see *JD*, 13:56). Thus we see how essential the holy scriptures are, for they teach us of these vital things that we may better develop our own character and faith.

2. See *TPJS*, p. 220.

3. In the Book of Mormon alone there are 3,471 references to the Savior (Susan Black's count)—see Robert J. Matthews, "What the Book

of Mormon Tells Us About Jesus Christ," in *The Book of Mormon: The Keystone Scripture,* Paul R. Cheesman, ed. (Provo: BYU Religious Studies Center, 1988), p. 33. Robert J. Matthews has found in the Book of Mormon a total of 86 names or designations that are used to refer to the Savior (see his "An Appreciation for the Book of Mormon," Ninth Annual Sidney B. Sperry Symposium, 24 January 1981, pp. 26–27).

4. *JD* 14:97.

5. In Kenneth W. Godfrey, Audrey M. Godfrey, and Jill Mulvay Derr, *Women's Voices* (Salt Lake City: Deseret Book Company, 1982), p. 147.

6. In *JD* 4:34.

7. In *JD* 7:230.

8. In George A. Smith letter of 20 October 1848 to Orson Pratt.

9. Recorded by E.M. Greene, clerk, at Kanesville, 5 November 1848.

10. *An Address to All Believers in Christ* (Richmond, Missouri, 1887), p. 8.

11. Lucy Cowdery Young letter of 7 March 1887 to Brigham Young (Church Archives).

12. *Improvement Era,* March 1912, pp. 418–19.

13. Leslie Crider Humphreys, "From Misery to Joy," *The Friend,* February 1995, pp. 45, 46.

14. *My First Mission* (Salt Lake City: Juvenile Instructor Office, 1882), pp. 67, 68.

15. Joseph Fielding Smith, *Life of Joseph F. Smith* (Salt Lake City: Deseret News Press, 1938), pp. 184, 187.

16. *Instant Memory: The Automatic Memory System* (Pacific Palisades, California: The Institute of Advanced Thinking, 1964), p. 3.

17. *Instant Memory,* p. 3.

18. Wayne Martindale and Jerry Root, eds., *The Quotable Lewis* (Wheaton, Illinois: Tyndale House Publishers, Inc., 1990), p. 424.

19. C.S. Lewis, *The Weight of Glory and Other Addresses* (Grand Rapids: Eerdmans Publishing Company, 1965), p. 5.

20. Joseph F. Smith, *Gospel Doctrine* (Salt Lake City: Deseret Book Company, 1977), p. 311.

Chapter 7
Following the Prophets

1. Gordon B. Hinckley, "Joseph the Seer," *Ensign,* May 1977, p. 64.

2. "Believe His Prophets," *Ensign,* May 1992, pp. 50, 51.

3. In "This Is the Work of the Master," *Ensign,* May 1995, pp. 69–70. At Ira's funeral President Seymour B. Young said of him that he was "a man who had never betrayed a trust, never betrayed his brethren

and never betrayed his God; a man who had scattered blessings along his pathway through life, not only to his loved ones, but to all with whom he came in contact."

4. Journal entry of 23 October 1857.

5. In *JD* 12:269–70.

6. In *JD* 8:16.

7. In *JD* 4:297.

8. In *JD* 8:292.

9. In *JD* 11:42. See also D&C 122:7.

10. Brigham Young's Office Journal, 28 January 1857.

11. In *JD* 6:148.

12. "Contend Not with Others, but Pursue a Steady Course," *Improvement Era*, June 1970, p. 41.

13. "Of You It Is Required to Forgive," *Ensign*, November 1980, p. 62.

14. Mark L. McConkie, *The Father of the Prophet* (Salt Lake City: Bookcraft, 1993), p. 77.

15. *Times and Seasons*, 5:649–50.

Chapter 8
Trying the Virtue of the Word of God

1. Brigham Young, in *JD* 8:115.

2. Brigham Young, in *JD* 7:275.

3. Their comparative usefulness and holiness nevertheless caused the Lord to choose ancient Israel "to be a special people . . . above all the people that are upon the face of the earth" (Deuteronomy 7:6).

4. William Law, *A Serious Call to a Devout and Holy Life* (Grand Rapids, Michigan: Sovereign Grace Publishers, 1971), p. 148.

5. In Hugh Nibley, *The World and the Prophets* (Salt Lake City and Provo: Deseret Book Co. and Foundation for Ancient Research and Mormon Studies, 1987), p. 16.

6. Bertrand Russell, "A Free Man's Worship," in *Mysticism and Logic and Other Essays* (New York: Longman, Green and Co., 1925), p. 57.

7. Robert Cooke, in *The Salt Lake Tribune*, 12 November 1995, p. A-1.

8. Marcel Proust, *The Captive*, trans. C. K. Scott Moncrieff (New York: The Modern Library, 1929), pp. 250–51.

9. In William Griffin, *Clive Staples Lewis: A Dramatic Life* (San Francisco: Harper and Row, 1986), p. 79.

10. Justin Martyr, quoted by Hugh Nibley in *The World and the Prophets*, p. 226.

11. Clement, Bishop of Rome, in *The Lost Books of the Bible* (New York: Bell Publishing Company, 1979), p. 130.

12. PBS production of Ford Madox Ford's *The Good Soldier.*

13. James Thompson, *The City of Dreadful Night and Other Poems* (London: Bertram Dobell, 1899), pp. 29–30, 35–36.

14. Nathaniel Hawthorne, *The English Notebooks,* ed. Randall Stewart (New York: Modern Language Association of America, 1941), pp. 432–33.

15. Dean of St. Paul's Cathedral, London, *Daily Express,* London, 13 July 1953, p. 4.

Chapter 9
Living in a Community of Saints

1. See Robert D. Putnam, "Bowling Alone: America's Declining Social Capital," *Journal of Democracy,* January 1995, pp. 69, 70, 73.

2. Putnam, "Bowling Alone," p. 75.

3. Alexis de Tocqueville, *Democracy in America,* Richard D. Heffner, ed. (New York: New American Library, 1956), p. 194.

4. George Santayana, as quoted in Anne Colby and William Damon, *Some Do Care* (New York: The Free Press, 1992), p. 1.

5. *Some Do Care,* pp. 296–97.

6. In *JD* 7:65.

7. *TPJS,* p. 195.

8. Eugene D. Genovese, "Pilgrim's Progress," *The New Republic,* 11 May 1992, p. 38.

9. In *JD* 5:207.

10. *Gospel Doctrine,* pp. 297–98.

Chapter 10
Witnessing for the Name of the Lord Jesus

1. *The Interpreter's Dictionary of the Bible* (New York: Abingdon Press, 1962), p. 500.

2. See LDS Bible Dictionary, p. 713.

3. See LDS Bible Dictionary, p. 633.

4. In *JD* 3:205–6.

5. See Boyd K. Packer, *That All May Be Edified* (Salt Lake City: Bookcraft, 1982), p. 337.

6. In *JD* 8:313.

7. *Doctrines of Salvation,* comp. Bruce R. McConkie, 3 vols. (Salt Lake City: Bookcraft, 1954–56), 1:44.

Chapter 11
Not Wearying by the Way

1. "If the Way Be Full of Trial, Weary Not," *Deseret Sunday School Songs* (Salt Lake City: Deseret Sunday School Union, 1909), no. 158.
2. Rudyard Kipling, in Charles Carrington, ed., *Rudyard Kipling: His Life and Work* (London: Macmillan, 1955), p. 575.
3. See *JD* 2:267.
4. In *JD* 11:25.
5. Ann Morrow Lindbergh, *Gift from the Sea* (New York: Vintage Books, 1975), p. 32.
6. Brigham Young, Nauvoo, 28 December 1843, from Wilford Woodruff journal.
7. Brigham Young, in *JD* 14:277.
8. Brigham Young, in *JD* 6:75.
9. Count de Falloux, ed., *The Writings of Madame Swetchine,* trans. H. W. Preston (Boston: Roberts Brothers, 1869), p. 7.
10. *The Teachings of Ezra Taft Benson* (Salt Lake City: Bookcraft, 1988), p. 396.

Chapter 12
Enduring It Well

1. George Q. Cannon, *Collected Discourses,* comp. Brian H. Stuy (Burbank, B.H.S. Publishing, 1988), 2:185.
2. "How Firm a Foundation," *Hymns,* 1985, no. 85.
3. *A Grief Observed* (New York: Bantam Books, 1978), pp. 25, 38.
4. Brigham Young, in *JD* 2:250–51.
5. In *JD* 19:97.
6. In *JD* 8:31.
7. Sarah Bradford, *Disraeli* (London: Weidenfeld and Nicolson, 1982), p. 209.
8. Heber C. Kimball sermon 8 January 1845, in minutes, Brigham Young Papers (Church Archives).
9. In *JD* 10:251.
10. See *JD* 5:115; 11:275.
11. In *JD* 7:204.

SUBJECT INDEX

Scripture Index

NEW TESTAMENT

BOOK OF MORMON

DOCTRINE AND COVENANTS

PEARL OF GREAT PRICE